Álvaro Siza

Álvaro Siza
Inside the City

preface by Álvaro Siza
text by Marc Dubois
photos by Giovanni Chiaramonte

Whitney Library of Design

An imprint of Watson-Guptill Publications/New York

Cover: Centro Gallego
de Arte Contemporáneo, 1988-93
(photo Giovanni Chiaramonte)

First published in the United States in 1998 by Whitney Library of
Design, an imprint of Watson-Guptill Publications,
a division of BPI Communications, Inc.,
1515 Broadway, New York, NY, 10036.

© 1996 Federico Motta Editore SpA
© 1998 Whitney Library of Design, English language edition

Original title: Álvaro Siza: Dentro la città

Direction
Pierluigi Nicolin

Editorial Supervision
Guia Sambonet

Design
Giorgio Camuffo / Gaetano Cassini

Translated from the Italian by Jay Hyams

Cataloging-in-Publication Data is on file with the Library of Congress.
ISBN: 0-8230-0171-7

Manufactured in Italy
First US printing, 1998

1 2 3 4 5 / 02 01 00 99 98

The materials in this book were
organized by Roberto Cremascoli.

The photographs are by
Giovanni Chiaramonte, except for those
on pages 20, 37, 38, 89, which are by
Teresa Siza, and pages 64-79, which
are by Lorenzo Mussi.

Thanks to Maria Teresa Conidi and
Edison Okumura for their contributions.

Preface Álvaro Siza

I recall attending the presentation of a public building that the architect described in the following way: "This is the town hall of a small medieval city now experiencing growth. The building is surrounded by smaller-size constructions. I broke up its volume in an effort to do nothing that would alter the preexisting scale."

I immediately thought of the skyline of Oporto: a large cube, its smooth sides perforated by windows arranged according to a regular rhythm, looming over the compact city. The contrast is violent. But the building in question—the bishop's palace—creates relationships with other, equally autonomous buildings (churches, monuments, theaters, soccer stadiums, convents, hospitals, libraries, bridges, museums).

A city's equilibrium, its comfort, and its very habitability depend on such contrasts, whether they are visually perceptible or only evoked in memory.

By their nature, towering buildings like that also depend on the relationships that come to be established between them and any topographical peculiarities, such as existing green areas, large or small, even if it's no more than a single tree, or with the sea, or with the long embankment constituted by a river. Regardless of the specific "conversation" between the "main characters" (those identifying gestures, the repeatedly exchanged signals, that chorus of voices whose volume swells ever larger), the unifying element of a city consists in a fabric of continuous and apparently banal constructions, composed of repetition and contrast, the very existence of which creates the necessity for monuments. When a city grows, and its town hall—the residence that belongs to all its citizens—comes to require a larger area, any attempt to conceal this involves the entire city. Extension of the constructed fabric alters the system of relationships; and perpetual movement governs and readjusts the city's balance.

The rhythms of this movement are different in New York or Amarante, but the movement itself always exists, as it exists between cities and regions, between the Natural and the Constructed. The activity of the architect is located within this continuous repositioning. A ballet, almost imperceptible but uninterrupted, takes place on the terrestrial surface, and those who fail to follow the movements of the chorus or those of the soloists cannot play a part: allegro, andante, adagio. An architect is no ballerina. But like any carpenter or electrician, like a director or even a simple walk-on performer without lines, the architect must be familiar with the work, must know when not to use too much light, or too little, must know how to avoid assuming an expression that is overdone or too subtle, must recognize the differences among all the many voices and gestures so as not to attribute equal weight when doing so would be in error. The craft is incompatible with the very notion of specialization—the notion of an architect specializing in town houses, an architect specializing in museums, an architect specializing in skyscrapers.

Almost all of us come to be stamped with a label denoting "expert" in some area or another, but only someone who has experience designing museums can truly design a town house, and vice versa.

Álvaro Siza Vieira *Marc Dubois*

The Fragility of Equilibrium   The work of Álvaro Siza Vieira is among the most fascinating of our age. The interest in his work that was awakened in the 1970s has never diminished over the years, a fact that in and of itself represents a true phenomenon. Critical essays make it abundantly clear that Siza's work does not fit neatly within the framework of any dogma or abstract concept and that searching for concrete theoretical guidelines within his work is futile, since that work is grounded firmly in the reality of life and in the relationships among the visible and invisible factors presented by each individual site and its proposed project.

Wilfried Wang made the fitting observation that as many talented architects age, the increasing importance of the commissions they are offered is accompanied by a commensurate narrowing of their vision, but in the case of Siza one can say that exactly the opposite has occurred. As his career has progressed, in fact, his sphere of references has continued to expand; and he has taken the most disparate influences and made them his own, fitting them into the complex process that designing is for him. In one of his best-known statements, Siza declared that designing does not mean creating something new but rather transforming something that already exists, by which he means reality.

This process of transformation is expressed by way of a network of unexpected connections, marked in turn by a high level of unpredictability. Siza does not work on the basis of reusable modules. He demonstrates no allegience to the purity of types and avoids all schematism. His approach involves bringing heterogeneous elements together and is based on a method that develops itself gradually and is designed to channel the diverse forces that interact in the architectural process. In his view, the architect acts as a kind of catalyst, because the architect looks on the reality of a culture, of a city, of a society as a kind of process of continuous transformation. In this sense it is essential to accept the alternation between construction and deconstruction.

There is something more in Siza, however, for he is capable of expressing the fragility and poetics of architecture with a kind of naturalness, as if, in a sense, these elements are created through spontaneous generation, involving no effort, whereas in reality anything new is invariably the outcome of difficult, painstaking labor.

The Scale of the Design   More sketches by Siza have been published than those of any other well-known architect at the international level, with the possible exception of Aldo Rossi. These sketches do not present idealized situations, but rather the outcomes of unresolved conflicts, so Siza's sketches are very different, say, from Erich Mendelsohn's efficient expositions or Louis Kahn's attempts to affix the ideal "form" to paper, to give but two examples. As for Rossi, his sketches serve several functions, including that of visualizing the transformation of the scale, but Siza's sketches show no trace of Rossi's solid expressiveness, with his dramatic flair for the use of color. Siza's fine geometric designs, from which color is totally absent, are first and foremost evidence that the plan is extremely labile, the expression of a series of doubts based on the accumulation of a series of conflicts. For Siza, the sketch is much the same as taking notes, and it never achieves individual autonomy; it is also the preferred means for reaching the best understanding of scale, the scale of a small object, of a large-size site, of an ambitious and complex project. It happens sometimes that in a series of sketches Siza will draw his own hands; that is meant to indicate that the process of transformation comes not only from the mind, but also in the course of actually designing, through the hands that transmit doubts to paper.

The Scale of References   Siza is an architect who travels without theoretical baggage; whether preparing a project for Berlin, for The Hague, for Venice, or for some other locality, he directs his attention to the characteristics of the site where he is to work before concerning himself with the building program or even the dimensions of the site itself. Although Siza is absolutely free of the almost obsessive drive to leave a personal imprint that is so characteristic of Mario Botta or Richard Meier, his works are recognizably his. Critics claim that the strong influence of Aalto is evident in his earliest creations, but as Siza's career has progressed, the gamut of available references has broadened, and today one can find in his work signs reminiscent of Oud, Wright, Loos, Le Corbusier, and many other great architects of this century, even though, typically, such signs are barely perceptible and have no appreciable effect on the final result.

The study of the different phases of working out a project, beginning with many sketches, reveals a tireless investigation of the *scale* of a building. In this regard, examination of the process that led to the birth of the building designed to house the faculty of architecture of Oporto is extremely interesting. In the period between the end of 1986 and the beginning of 1987, Siza planned a massive architectural structure, closed off and furnished with a large internal patio, an idea clearly inspired by the bishop's palace designed by the architect Mazzoni, which stands in the same city and is a dominant part of the city's skyline. The sketch includes one variation of a building with a U-shaped ground plan overlooking the valley of the Douro River; the volume opens to the east, maintaining the U shape and at the same time creating an architectural mass overlooking a beautiful garden where two other faculty buildings stand. At this point, the various studios are grouped in an arrangement that looks something like a comb, but in later versions they are gradually transformed into independent towers that Siza, exploiting the unevenness of the terrain, connects by means of structures buried halfway in the ground. The creation of independent towers also makes it possible to view the valley from the largest of the structures, the one that hosts the auditoriums and library; the northern side of this structure is without openings so as to serve as a kind of screen against the noise pollution from the nearby highway. The most unexpected form is the semicylindrical volume located in front of the exhibition space; the layout of this area is in several respects similar to the exhibition hall of the fine arts museum of Ghent, which Siza had the opportunity to see in October 1987, at the same time that he was beginning to dedicate himself completely to the Oporto project. It's fascinating to see how elements casually discovered during the course of his many travels end up being as part of his own work. With regard to the independent pavilions, the references to the iconography and configurative typology typical of the residences designed by Adolf Loos have been reported many times, and Wilfried Wang sees the work as a sort of "Portuguese Acropolis," in which the dining hall corresponds to the Temple of Nike. The open access structure, a small portico, recalls the portico designed by Le Corbusier for the building in Paris known as "La Cité de Refuge" of the Salvation Army.

Far more important than trying to identify the various possible influences in his work is to realize that Siza increasingly relies on hybridizations of heterogeneous elements, which at some point become the regulating principle of the project. Hans van Dijk emphasizes that Siza follows the "ordering sensibility of heterotopia," a regulating principle that involves the union of elements which are of equivalent importance but which do not lead back to one another and can never be fused. His work also constitutes a direct appeal for a version of architecture in which the sensory is not neglected but is rather used as the point of departure for a project. This can be seen in both the small building that is a bank headquarters in Vila do Conde (1982) and in one of his masterpieces, the Quinta de Malagueira quarter of Évora, which he has been working on since 1977. This last project goes far beyond the boundaries of an abstract urban concept. Here, Siza has exploited areas of unevenness in the terrain and various characteristics specific to the setting with enormous delicacy while at the same time creating visual connections with the skyline of the historic center of Évora; it is a thoroughly convincing demonstration that stimulation of the senses is an indispensable prerequisite for achieving results this striking. The effect is not really a matter of scale, but reflects a feeling that what is tiny is as important as what is large, a conviction that both must be treated with respect.

[Siza as Designer]
On a Reduced Scale   Siza began his career in a brilliant enough manner with the Boa Nova restaurant in Leça de Palmeira (1958-63), designing all of the restaurant's interior space also, even its furniture and lamps. With this project he demonstrated his enormous sensitivity for all aspects of his field—from the location of the building in its rocky setting to the final touches to the lighting fixtures. No one would ever call Siza an "industrial designer." Rather, he designs objects as if by chance, which are then made in limited series. Only during the last few years, the period of many large-scale public commissions, has he been asked to design small objects for everyday use. One of the most fascinating of these is an ashtray called the "Havana," which is designed more for use with a large cigar than for cigarettes. The Havana is made of glass or crystal in various colors, and the basic shape is that of a

"Havana" ashtray

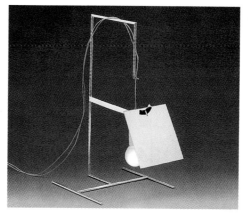

"Fil" lamp

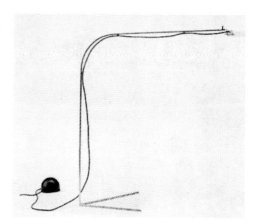

"Flamingo 1972" lamp

perfect half-sphere, with a small notch. When the object is flat side up, it seems to be in a state of unstable equilibrium, and its relative stability increases or decreases, depending on circumstances. When the object is turned over, however, it becomes a solid, strongly sensual form.

This instability is characteristic of objects designed by Siza, most of which are also extremely delicate. Regardless of the scale he's working in, from the smallest object to the largest public building, Siza seems always to want to express some lingering doubt and at the same time to disguise it. The small lamp designed for the Mobles 144 company ("Fil") is based on an purely minimalist concept, but is by no means a sophisticated technical product. Still later he designed a lamp called "Flamingo 1972," a name meant to evoke the long legs of that elegant bird. More than a source of illumination, it is an expression of doubt and surprise engendered by the fact that a creation like this can actually stand. The vision that Siza expresses in such designs is in perfect accordance with his vision of architecture as a union of hybrid elements leading to the creation of something thoroughly unusual. Even so, no one would claim that his small-scale creations are pioneering; in reality, they represent the demystification of a design approach, or tendency. What Siza creates is something different from what we generally understand by the term "industrial design," and he gives a highly personal interpretation to the concept of minimalist design, at the same time making an unexpected connection to his own architecture. The fragility that invariably distinguishes his architectural designs can be said to reach its highest expression in these small objects, and

this is why one can say of Siza that the concerns of the artisan always far outweigh any sense of the technological.

[The water tower of Aveiro]
On an Enlarged Scale   When the new campus of the University of Aveiro was being planned, several architects, members of the group commonly referred to as the Oporto school, were contacted. Siza was entrusted with designing not just the new library but also a water tower, a type of construction considered standard within the sphere of civil architecture. The design he presented for this tower is very different from the usual idea of a water tower, which is based on its function—to house an internal structure, most often a circular tank. Siza's version, before being anything else, is an object placed within a landscape. There is a concrete tank, but it stands on a supporting panel and a hollow column, also of concrete. Almost all structures of this type look the same from any angle; Siza presents the viewer with a vertical structure that takes on a different form according to the angle from which it is viewed. The asymmetry of the composition gives it a sense of instability and fragility that one doesn't expect in a structure of this kind.

The water tower seems to have more in common with the small objects Siza has designed than with any large-scale architectural project, and the tension between the supporting panel and the column recalls the form of an object designed by the Italian designer Achille Castiglioni in 1989, the "Joy," which was described as a "mobile with rotating shelves." Analysis of Castiglioni's works leads to the conclusion that he, like Siza, incorporates a great many different influences in the intense process of transformation that is design. Such work invariably incorporates openings to entire series of stimuli, requiring the viewer's constant attention and leading one not only to look at objects but to actually see them.

The Private Residence   In the work of some architects, such as James Stirling or Jean Nouvel, the private residence hardly appears at all; such is not true of Siza, who has always considered the design of private homes a compelling and irresistable challenge that permits him to achieve results of great intensity. For Siza, direct discussions with the future inhabitants are of enormous value, since they permit him to keep in close contact with the very essence of living within a space.

Many critics have called attention to Siza's ability to incorporate the visible and invisible lines of force characteristic of a given site within a design. A compelling example of this is the way in which the faculty of architecture in Oporto is "anchored" to the slope overlooking the Douro River. With private homes, however, the situation is often quite different. In the enlargement of the Alcino Cardoso house (1971–73), the scale of the new building is still determined by the interaction between the terrain and the preexisting construction, but in other cases Siza has found himself entrusted with the design of buildings in suburban areas, sometimes on expanses of ground devoid of interesting natural features. In his design of the Beires home in Póvoa de Varzim, Portugal (1973–76), one of the corners of the architectural mass has been broken off, and the surface of the break has been transformed into a complex glassed-in façade on which all the most important rooms converge: In this project orientation is of primary importance, with the interior being transformed into a space opened outward.

In the case of the Avelino Duarte home in Ovar (1981–85), the rectangular lot on which the house was to be built offered no useful point of departure, so Siza decided to design the building as something autonomous. Seen from outside, the home looks like a plain white cube with no openings, but its interior reveals a spatial layout that is both unexpected and fascinating. Not surprisingly, many people have compared this design to Adolf Loos and his *Raumplan;* the connections to Loos become even clearer when one considers the way the front and back

façades narrow toward the top and when one notes the use of marble slabs facing on interior walls along with mirrors to obtain a spatial displacement. However, there are striking differences in terms of the way Loos typically organized space; in fact, the classic *Raumplan* is always based on the relationships among adjacent spaces that are characterized by ceilings at different heights.

There is something else in the Duarte house, too: Just past the main door, one enters an atrium that is three floors high and illuminated by natural light entering by way of the ceiling. The placement of such a large space inside a house is in many ways similar to the Van Eetvelde Row House in Brussels designed by Victor Horta in the Art Nouveau style. The dimensions of the space and its placement directly past the entryway make clear references to the arrangement employed by Le Corbusier in the La Roche House in Paris. If the house is viewed in cross section, one can see how its sense of space is reinforced by a clearly defined diagonal line visually linking the first floor to the third. Standing at the center of the building on the second floor one can see both the sky and the garden at the same time—the sky from a window in the upper façade, the garden from a window on the ground floor. Siza was not content to merely give the house an increased *sense* of open space, but also used that design element to introduce an almost imperceptible system of natural ventilation for the bedrooms.

In the Duarte home Siza succeeded in taking a compact volume and placing within it an interior on a markedly different scale. In the garden behind the house are two other independent volumes; one of them is designed to serve as a garage, the other as a doghouse. The white cube made to be used as a doghouse might seem like an unimportant detail had Siza not repeated it in his design for the upper school in Setúbal (1986–94), where the same idea of an independent, accessory volume is used for a structure than can be used as a guest house or custodian's residence. This construction is a particularly noteworthy example of Siza carrying foward the principle of the enlargement of scale in an unusual manner, yet it is mentioned only rarely in the many publications devoted to the Setúbal project.

From Private Homes to Public Housing   After his first important foreign commission, which took him to Berlin, where he worked on the plans to renovate the Kreuzberg quarter, Siza was invited to work on a project for the commune of The Hague. Having contributed to SAAL projects in Oporto immediately after the Revolution of the Carnations in 1974, Siza had rapidly made a name for himself in Europe as an architect with a particular skill at involving future inhabitants in building plans. For him, such participation inevitably opens the door to innumerable conflicts, but in Berlin he had already proven that his works are not only the result of his careful study of scale and the architecture of the city in which the buildings will stand, but also of his listening skills.

The first two building complexes of The Hague, called "Period" and "Comma" (1985–88), have 106 apartments. The project fits perfectly into the structure and the architecture of the late-19th-century quarter in terms of both scale and architectural weight. The buildings stand out from the others and at the same time blend with them, and the possible pitfall of monotony is avoided by creating small variations in the façades, making changes, for example, in the shape of the windows or in the color of the bricks used. Siza had no intention of making a dramatic change in the existing character of the site, nor did he hope to incorporate a highly personalized structure, something comparable to a foreign body, in a quarter already suffering from deterioration; rather, he followed the alignment of the other buildings, decided without a moment's hesitation to use bricks, and in fact—to the great surprise of many Dutch architects—reintroduced the traditional style of portico. The use of an external stairway running diagonally across the front façade, making it possible to enter apartments on the upper floors directly from the street, had once been widespread in popular housing in Holland, but had been abandoned with the birth of Dutch modernism. Siza reinterpreted the concept of the portico, once again proving himself dedicated to the close study of the specific characteristics of local architecture. Examination of the typical architecture of The Hague did not lead to a nostalgic recreation of the past, but rather to a process of transformation in which existing strengths were imbued with new life. Anyone familiar with architectural vocabularies will recognize the particular elements employed—such as the shape of the corners, marked by a certain fragility—and will immediately note the ingenuity of

the design, worked out to meet the specific needs of the future inhabitants, most of whom are from various ethnic minorities, but in large part from Islamic cultures. In general, this project stands as of one of the most fascinating within the sphere of urban renewal in Holland during the 1980s, and the positive response it received led to Siza being offered another project, this one for the Schilder quarter.

Siza devoted just as much intensive study to the plans for this second site as he had to the first, and the final result fits perfectly into the existing context while at the same time transforming it. Wilfried Wang points out that in the design of this project Siza must have consciously decided to emphasize the relationship between the building complex and the street, such that the result, looked at in terms of setting, is very much in keeping with the urban schemes worked out by the city agencies. Instead of a single complex on Jacob van Campen Square, Siza opted for two smaller volumes, and on Jacob Cat Street he reduced the building to three floors; by means of these adjustments he divided the entire project into two parts: a linear building with four floors, a flat roof, and square windows; and a building of three floors with a pitched roof and rectangular windows. By analogy with the residential projects designed by the famous Dutch architect Berlage, the severe lines of the façades terminate at the corners in highly expressive architectonic elements. A sense of unity is achieved by the uniform use of brick of a dark red color; and the narrow volumes placed on the ends of the structures with pitched roofs overlooking Van Campen Square also create visual continuity. Using such measures, none particularly draamatic taken by itself, Siza succeeds in refining the scale of this large project, placing it within the rich tradition of Dutch popular housing. This is not a radical restructuring but rather a respectful contribution to a residential setting of great quality.

At about the same time that Siza was working on the first of these large commissions, he was designing two houses for the custodians of Van der Venne Park, which is also located in the Schilder quarter. In the design for those homes, he once again demonstrated his preference for the hybridization of formal languages. The two homes, located above a garage, also reveal his ability to turn freeeedom of choice in building materials to his advantage. One of the two houses has walls of whitewashed plaster; the walls of the other are red brick. The red brick walls are without openings, while those of the plaster house facing south have windows and terraces. The two buildings are connected to each other by way of a series of structural motifs—for example, the brick balustrade is continued beneath the white building—and in this way Siza successfully blends the two elements in a unexpected way that becomes a sort of homage to Dutch residential architecture, a happy marriage between New Objectivity and the Amsterdam school. He synthesizes, albeit on a reduced scale, the two leading currents in Dutch architecture of the twenties and thirties; and unlike other, similar creations, in which references to the recent past of modern architecture are pushed into the background, here those references are abundantly clear. The project exemplifies a technique in which recognizable elements are combined in order to create a composition which offers both a sense of fragments and of partially crystallized images that appear in a variety of different configurations, and it is precisely this technique which Siza takes to its highest expression in the small project for this park.

[The Reconstruction of the Chiado District]
The Strategy of Memory   In August 1988 an enormous fire swept through the section of downtown Lisbon known as the Chiado district, damaging or destroying many buildings. The loss of part of the city's historic center caused widespread consternation, and Siza was immediately called in to formulate a plan for the reconstruction of the district. His proposal, adopted in 1990 and carried out in several phases, followed the general wish on the part of the population to maintain the district's original appearance. The façades of the buildings, those that remained standing and those that had been destroyed, were carefully restored or rebuilt, preserving the original architectural styles, and Siza did nothing to change the height of the buildings and their arrangement, which he restored so they were just as they had been in the past. Siza had no intention of making drastic changes to a site of such historic importance simply to express some personal whim, and would certainly never have introduced a foreign element that would not match the scale of the surrounding structures; nor would the plan he presented be an example of "window dressing," in which there

is a marked difference between the style of the exteriors and the style of the interiors.

In truth, the project involves something more than a mere reconstruction; to outward appearances, everything seems to have remained intact, but in reality the district was totally reworked, with major improvements being made. Siza's concept takes into account the complex mix of different functions within the area, yet at the same time makes the area's use as a residential zone a priority. By clearing out the interior courtyards, originally occupied by buildings, and making those interior areas accessible to the public, he created a different sense of scale within the fabric of the urban center. His dedication to proper scale is here expressed in the creation of new connections between Baixa and Bairro Alto and in the creation of new pedestrian routes using stairs and inclined ramps to offer pedestrians a completely different experience within the urban space. Thus in this project, Siza also emphasized the area's use as a public space.

[The Administration Building of the University of Alicante]
The Scale of Anchorage   The new campus of the University of Alicante was built on the site of a former military airport, a site totally outside of the context of nearby urban structures. Siza designed a building with an H-shaped floor plan for the new administration building, but the site's lack of any characteristics that needed to be accommodated in the design was itself in large part responsible for the direction the project took. The portion around the large patio matches the size and stepped structure of the nearby buildings that house the classrooms, but the most representative area repeats the elegance of the old control tower, a truly beautiful modernist construction. The scale of the buildings immediately around the new administration building offered a starting point for the project, but in no sense determined its style.

The basic concept is very similar to Siza's design for the upper school of Setúbal (1986–94), one of his most important projects to date. The decision to place all of the offices along two wings such that they face on to an elongated patio is identical, and the almost complete absence of openings in the exterior walls and the use of a long hall in each wing to connect the various offices to one another are also elements shared with the earlier design. In fact, at Setúbal Siza had already demonstrated his ability to establish the proper scale for these two long halls, a scale that he then marked off in a subtle way through the rhythmic use of zenithal lighting. The absence of openings in the external walls does much to emphasize the length of the wings of the administration building, but here this absence is as much a logical response to climatic conditions as it is a result of the desire to create a horizontal shape. Comparison of the two projects reveals other subtle changes: At Setúbal, only the main entrance and splendid atrium are located in the central area of the building, and the gymnasium and auditorium/great hall do not have a symmetrical relationship to that area. In Alicante, on the other hand, Siza put the great hall in a central position, its semicylindrical shape giving it a strikingly monumental sense. It is interesting to note how the project's single curved wall is made to serve as a kind of prelude to the building's two main entrances. Several architectural volumes are arranged around the great hall so as to create a second patio with a completely different scale and characteristics from the main patio. At first glance, this project may seem to have been characterized by greater practicality than the Setúbal project, but as he does so often Siza was probably using this reworking as an opportunity to introduce elements that confer a more strikingly poetic dimension to the whole.

[In the Name of the Shell]
Santiago de Compostela   Although located in a far corner of Europe, the sanctuary of Santiago de Compostela in Spain has occupied a position of enormous importance in Western culture for well over a thousand years. The Museum of Contemporary Art in Santiago de Compostela (1988–93) is not only the first large museum designed by Siza but also one of his most successful designs to date. A visit to the site reveals far more than can be gleaned from any photographs; the relationship between the scale of the surrounding buildings and the museum and the enormous wealth of stratified levels that Siza created in this project can be fully appreciated only through direct physical experience. Few other buildings in Europe succeed in being so subtly yet effectively integrated into such a rich historical context while at the same time sustaining a sense of their autonomous existence.

The widespread use of granite and the compact shapes of the buildings in the center of Santiago offered an essential departure point for Siza, but the specific nature and complexity of the site itself should not be overlooked. Without actually seeing the building, however, it is very difficult to comprehend the basic decisions behind the project and to appreciate its true scale. The new museum stands on part of the area of the ancient convent of Santo Domingo de Bonaval, a historic complex sometimes used for exhibitions, bordering a large garden surrounded by a wall. To avoid giving up the green space, Siza chose to build the new museum on the border of the garden, in the immediate vicinity of the convent, and integrated the building in the long wall surrounding the public park. The museum is shaped like a V; one of the two volumes follows the alignment of the adjacent buildings, and the other makes the building into a sort of wedge between the exterior of the enclosure and the preexisting historical building. This application of a wedge shape shows up in even the earliest sketches; the specific spatial scale and the way in which natural light is made to penetrate the two wings of the building were worked out in later sketches. Siza decided against the impressive "intermediate" structure suggested by the first sketches, and opted instead for a passageway that is at the same time separate and complex. Siza offers two ways, in two totally different scales, of reaching the museum's main entrance: a ramp and a staircase. The ramp can be taken as a metaphor for modernism. A fundamental element in Le Corbusier's "architectural promenade," it is a motif that Siza had already successfully employed in the complex of the faculty of architecture of Oporto. Anyone analyzing Siza's work from the point of view of the movement of the individual in space must reach the conclusion that he has developed a highly refined skill, comparable to that of Carlo Scarpa. This is not merely a matter of controlling the spatial configuration itself, but of having the ability to conceptualize the variations in scale that take place as the viewer perceives the configurations when moving about physically in space.
Climbing the stairs, one sees first of all a small projecting building with a square window: When one approaches the window to look in, one sees not only the cafeteria but also an area of the garden behind the building, including the long, narrow path that leads to a monumental tree. The window thus serves

not only to illuminate the ground floor and lower level, but becomes a picture frame for the historical garden. The angled slope of this detail of the building might be explained as a way to provide visibility to the people climbing the stairs, but the same slope is continued inside the building, where it is fully exploited. This is an illustrative example of how Siza combines spatial solutions and perceptive elements in a creation that at first seems merely formal.

Inside the building, Siza works out the sense of space based on variations in scale that are articulated through a series of exhibition spaces of very different types one from the next. The device he employs to make the visual connection between the foyer and the stairwell cannot be seen in a photograph; making use of the relationships among the varying scales, he exploits the unevenness of the ceiling, an important element of space that, in his opinion, architects neglect far too often. In the upper rooms, in which natural light enters indirectly through the zenith, he has adopted a truly unusual motif, attaching upside-down tables to the ceiling. The table, clearly a metaphor for architecture itself, goes from being a piece of furniture to being an architectural element defining space.

Much of the roof has been transformed into an open-air exhibition space. High granite walls surround a space made for the display of works of sculpture; the first sculpture was designed and set in place by Siza himself. This is a steep pyramid open on its less visible face so that natural light can pass through it to reach the hallway beneath it. This is far more than a mere skylight, however, and like the pyramid by Jože Plečnik that stands in the garden of the castle of Prague, it has a shape that recalls that of bell towers. Or was Siza instead inspired by the pyramid of Caius Cestius that stands against the thick Roman walls erected by Aurelian? In truth, the precise reference that Siza had in mind when he decided to build this pyramid is of little importance, although no doubt his work will offer a fecund field for the research of future art historians who set about trying to reconstruct the multitude of references found in them.

Siza's involvement was not limited to the building, for when the decision was made to restore the garden, which had fallen into near ruin, he assumed the role of "surveyor," carrying out the necessary innovations with infinite discretion, showing scrupulous respect for the peculiarities of the site and the terrain. His concept and conduct have nothing in common with the typical garden designer's grandiose or overintellectual approach. He used the unevenness of the terrain to make the walls seem to slowly rise from the ground, an idea he had already applied in his first work, the Boa Nova restaurant, and in the pool of Leça da Palmeira. The forms and reliefs of the terrain are further emphasized by the erection of geometric, linear walls. The sensitivity Siza showed in this operation has a close affinity with the sensitivity that Fernando Távora, his teacher and close friend, demonstrated in his design for the Quinta da Conceiçao park near Oporto (1956-60).

When he was a boy, Siza came with his parents to Santiago, a city whose symbol, the St. James scallop, is very much in evidence. Half a century later he gave a new building, unique in its genre, to that very city, a place of considerable historical importance. Perhaps it was written in the stars of the sky above Compostela that this man named Vieira, a word that means "St. James scallop" in Spanish, would have that special opportunity. The museum is itself a kind of shell, in the sense that its hard outer covering of granite gives no indication of what rests within its body. At first glance, Siza's building might seem like an intrusion, the result of an arrogant desire to set one's creation down in front of a protected historical structure, so that it, too, could be protected. In reality, Siza's museum represents both a kind of integration, an expression of both contrast and harmony between old and new, and the reassambling and outpouring, for this preordained site, of a multitude of elements which already existed in the immediate area or were collected by Siza on his long rambles through the city. The museum of Santiago, like all his works, is a creation based on profound respect and love, for as Siza has himself said about his works, "The strongest drive is always the quest for serenity."

Tower

Aveiro

Water Tower, Aveiro

This water tower, which serves the university campus, is composed of a tank made of reinforced concrete shaped like a parallelepiped supported by a concrete panel fifteen centimeters thick and a hollow concrete column. The two vertical elements are joined by two steel tie beams that ensure the stability of the structure. The column houses the tubing and also stairs, which are reached through a sturdy door of copper. The structure towers over the low lagoon area of Aveiro like a minimalist sculpture.

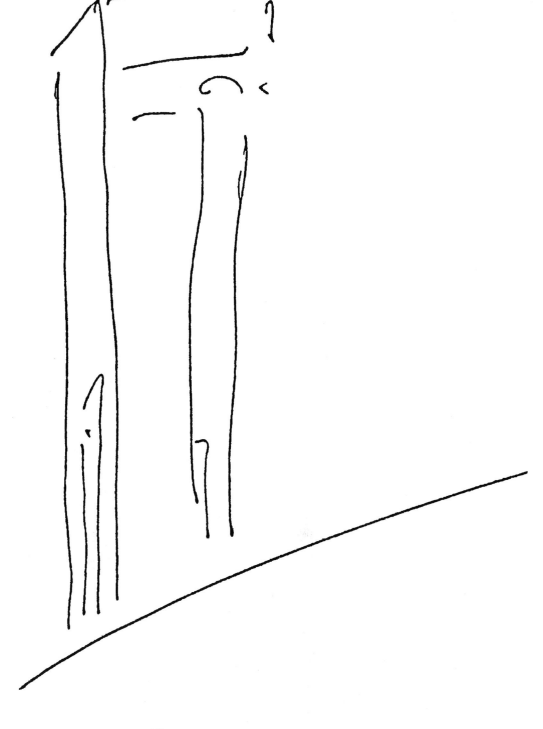

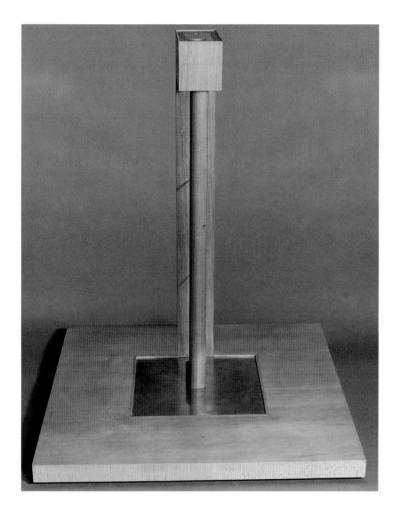 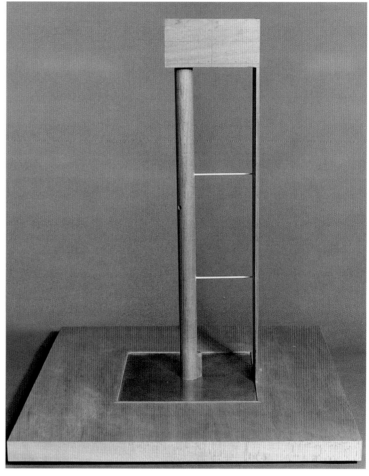

Views of the scale model (above).

Elevations, diagrams, and cross sections of the
first and second versions of the project (opposite).

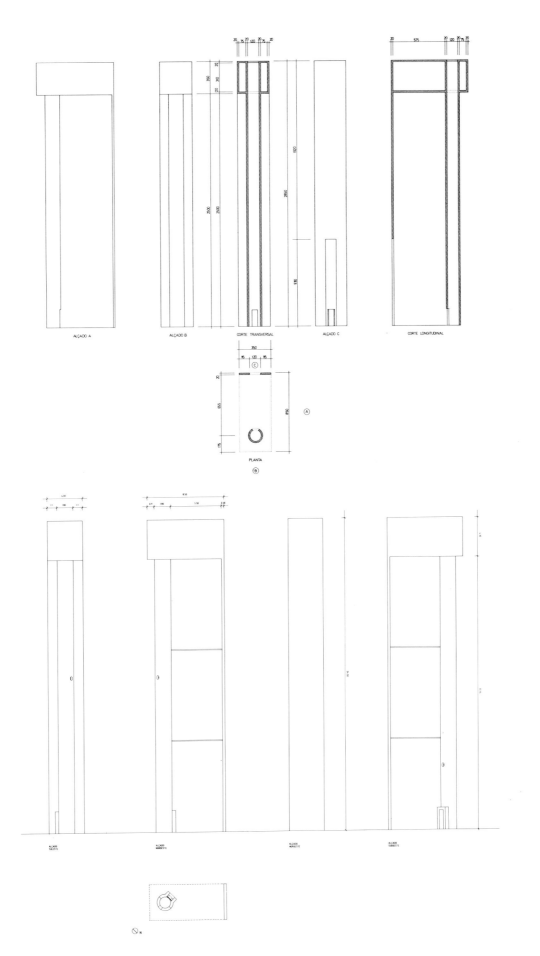

ALÇADO A   ALÇADO B   CORTE TRANSVERSAL   ALÇADO C   CORTE LONGITUDINAL

PLANTA

ALÇADO SUESTE   ALÇADO NOROESTE   ALÇADO NOROESTE   ALÇADO SUDESTE

N

The tower seen from various angles.

Ovar

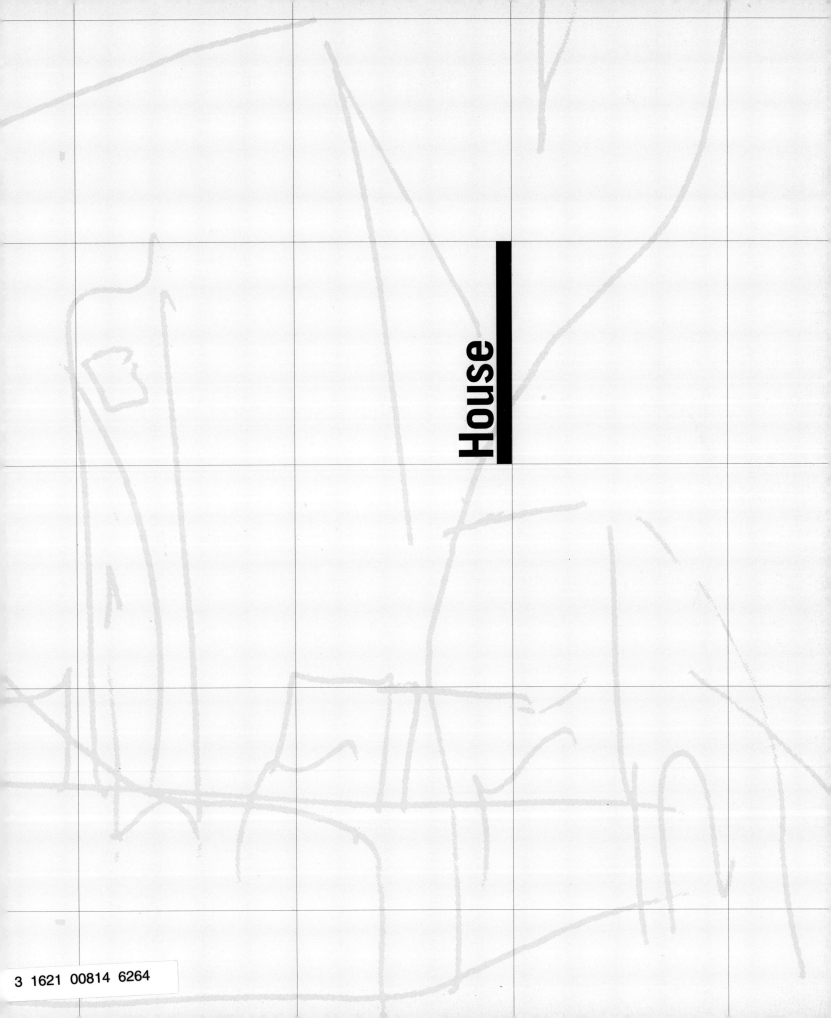

House

Avelino Duarte House, Ovar

This house occupies a rectangular lot on a tree-lined avenue in a suburb of this small Portuguese city, which is located to the south of Oporto. The structure is composed of the combination of three simple volumes arranged to create three floors, all of them joined by a vertical rectangular "excavation" opened in the front wall that forms the main entrance. The articulation of the volumes and their roofing is accomplished following a continuous operation of addition and subtraction using transitional elements between the interior and the exterior. The vaulted covering of the central body gives it emphasis. A fourth, smaller volume rests against the west wall, breaking the regular scheme of the layout (a-b-a-b), creating the second-floor loggia, and housing, and on the ground floor, the kitchen and laundry. With explicit reference to the Steiner House by Adolf Loos (1910), the exterior's bare simplicity contrasts sharply with the richness of the interior spaces, the inventiveness in their arrangement, and the materials used as wall coverings. Loos's *Raumplan* is evoked by the rhythm of the landings and the finishing of the marble stairs on the three floors; the use of a collage of precious materials is most evident in the ground-floor living room, where the marble facing of the fireplace and the isolated columns blend with the polished mirrors on the walls and the coping and the dark mahogany floors. The rooms on the second floor form two independent units connected by studies, box rooms, and short halls. The two bathrooms can be entered from the bedrooms or from the box rooms, thanks to pivoting doors arranged on a right angle. The large study/library on the third floor, which looks on to the front terrace, is illuminated by a window in the curved back of the "excavation" in the rear façade.

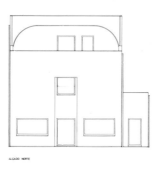

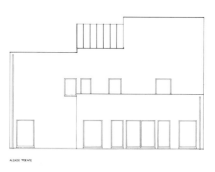

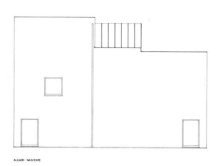

Side elevations (right) and views of the front with the main entrance (left and opposite).

Plan of the ground
and first floors.
Legend:
1 entrance
2 living room
3 fireplace
4 kitchen
5 rooms

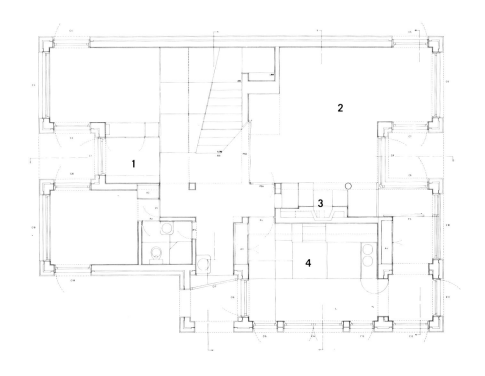

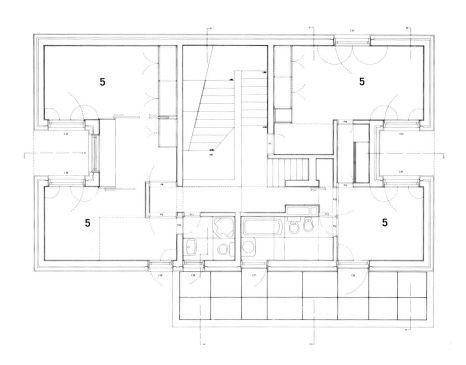

The stairs (right).
The west side with the loggia (below).

The wall coverings in marble and mirrors around
the fireplace (opposite top).
Section, layout, and elevation of the corner with
fireplace (opposite bottom).

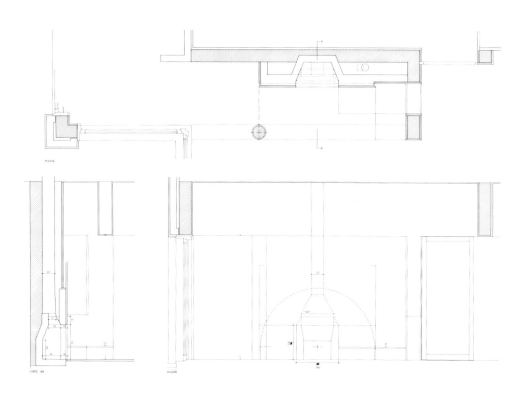

The stairway (above).
Longitudinal and cross sections (below).

The study/library on the third floor (opposite).

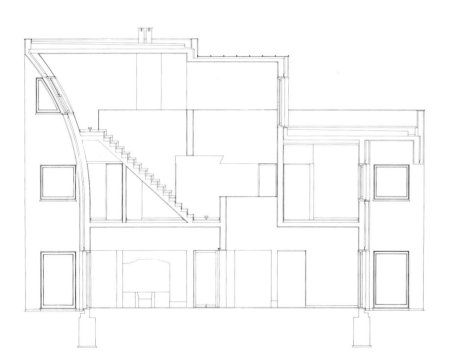
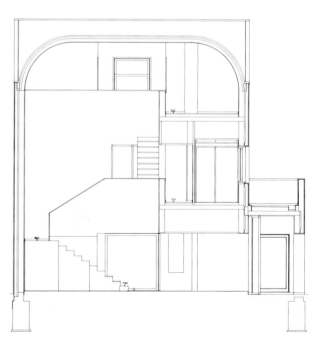

Alicante

University

University Administration Building, Alicante

The University of Alicante, in the city of San Vicente del Raspeig, occupies the area of the old Rabasa military airfield. The administration building marks the western edge of the campus, and its striking sense of horizontality distinguishes it from the many open spaces around it within the university enclosure. It stands on a rectangular plot of land between the complex of classroom buildings and the old control tower, a beautiful modernist construction. The width and stepped structure of the project are based on the classroom buildings; its compact, elegant volumes are a reflection of the nearby tower. The absence of openings on the exterior walls—a defense against the torrid climate in the style of Hispano-Muslim fortresses—and the austere, uniform character of the building emphasize its institutional importance. The structure, on two staggered floors, is in the shape of an H. The large patio to the south is for the administrative offices and the archives of the various faculties; the smaller patio is for public affairs offices (press office, rooms for video conferences, etc.); the semicircular building in the center of this space houses the auditorium/great hall. The body separating the two patios, illuminated from above by a skylight that symbolically unites the two floors, is used for horizontal and vertical connections and services (atrium, reception, etc.).

The main entrance to the administration building is located in the area of the control tower, on the south side in the single-floored part of the complex, and is aligned with the project's axis. This entrance is a sort of passageway—similar to the labyrinthine entrances to ancient Arab constructions, even including a fountain—and it leads, almost by surprise, to the large patio, the entire length of which must be crossed to reach the transverse

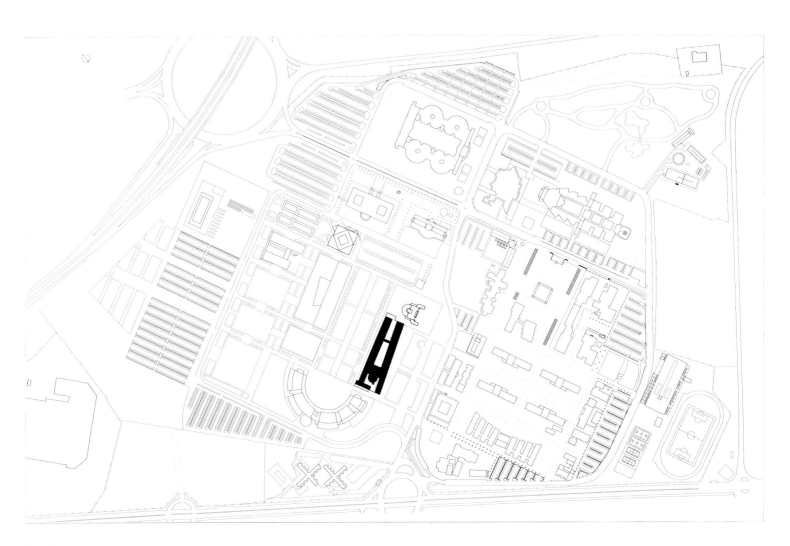

General layout.

(of the H) and the doors giving entry to the building. There are also two secondary entrances at the far other end, toward the classroom buildings. The first of these, for pedestrians, leads to the atrium; the second, made for vehicles, leads to the underground parking areas, the general archive, the storerooms, and the systems plant. The arrangement of the interior spaces, repeated across the entire length of the building, is based on a series of rooms that faces the patio in one direction and opens on to a long hall in the other. The rooms are separated from the hall by a double wall that contains the air-conditioning system.

The strictly institutional activities of the administration are located on the second floor. The offices of the vice-rectors and the rooms for the various other administrators are located above their respective departments and open on to the balcony over the large patio. Vertical connections between floors are made by way of two stairways that close off the wings of the second floor at the southern end. The council chamber is in the northeast wing of the small patio on the second floor. At the far opposite end, toward the campus, are the offices of the rector. The rector's offices have a large balcony facing outward; this is the only outward-looking element of the entire project, and thus serves to identify the part of the building that represents the most authority.

The framework for the construction is composed of pillars and beams, and double brick walls for insulation to protect the building from inclement weather. The outer walls are of plastered crushed earthenware and are protected by a stone socle 1.8 meters high, with the exception of the large patio; there, in keeping with regional tradition, they are dressed with the painted and glazed pottery tiles known as azulejos, which serve to keep the rooms cool.

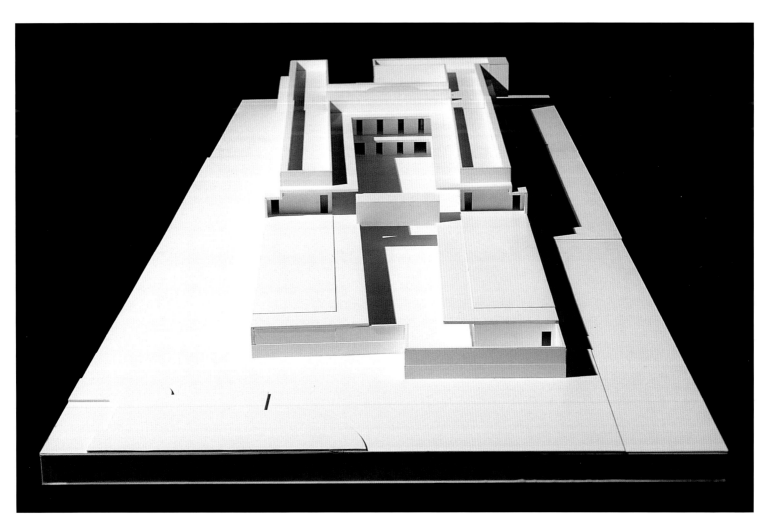

View of the scale model.

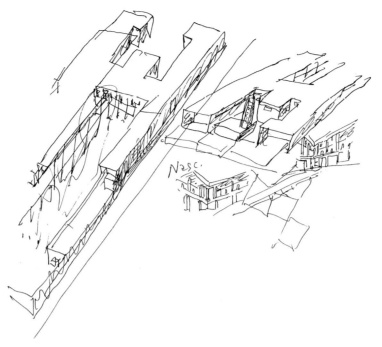

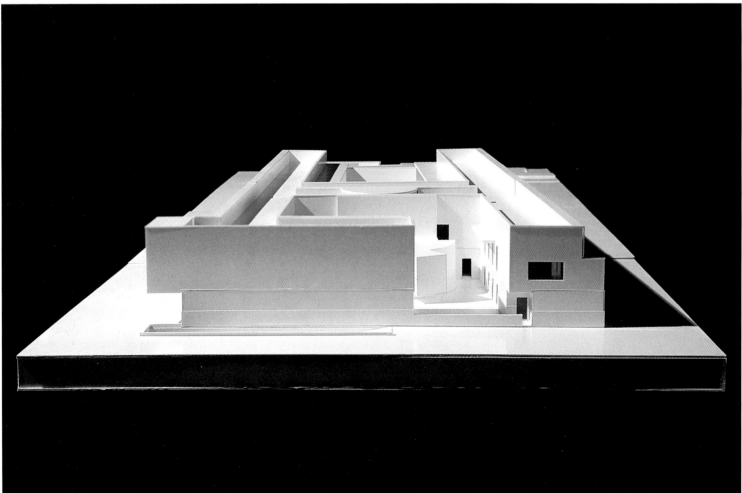

View of the scale model.

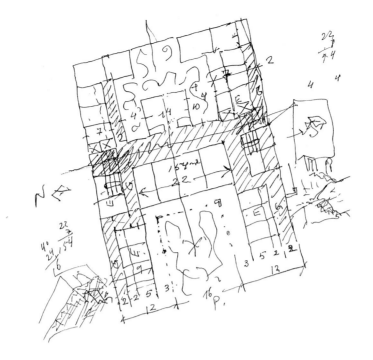

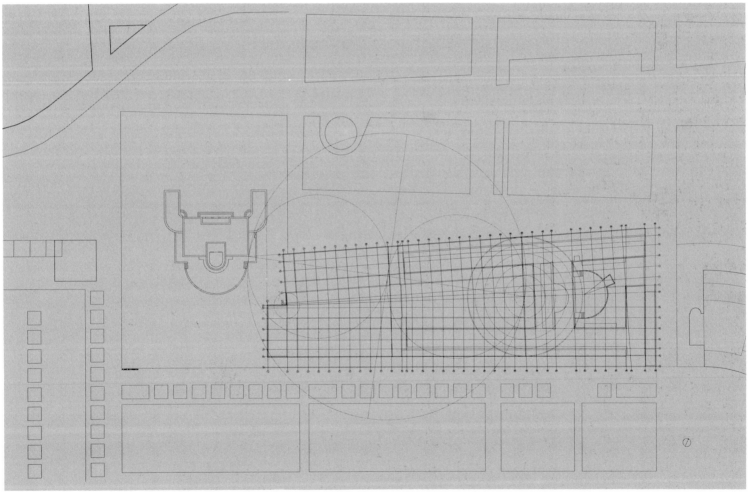

Roof plans, with project geometry.

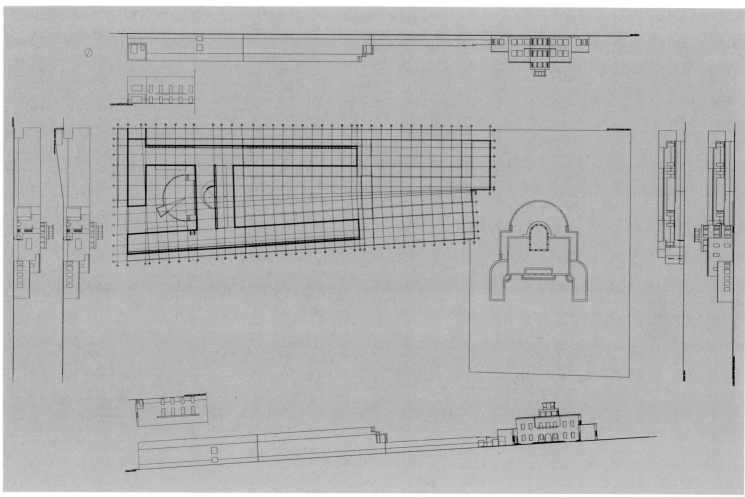

Roof plans (height above ground level
7.8 meters and 8.8 meters) and side elevations.

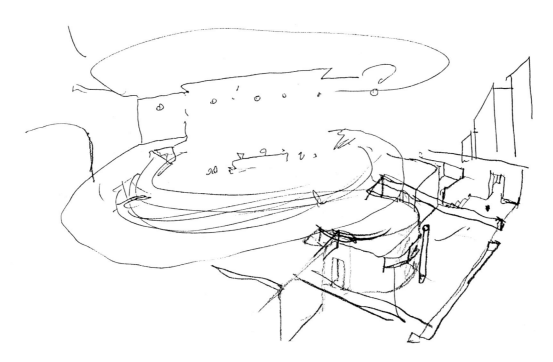

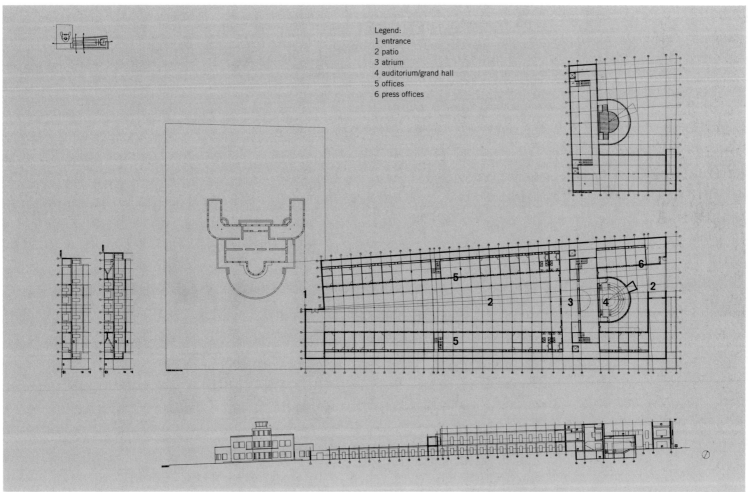

Legend:
1 entrance
2 patio
3 atrium
4 auditorium/grand hall
5 offices
6 press offices

Ground floor plan (height above ground level
0.3 meters) and basement plan (height below
ground level -3 meters) and sections.

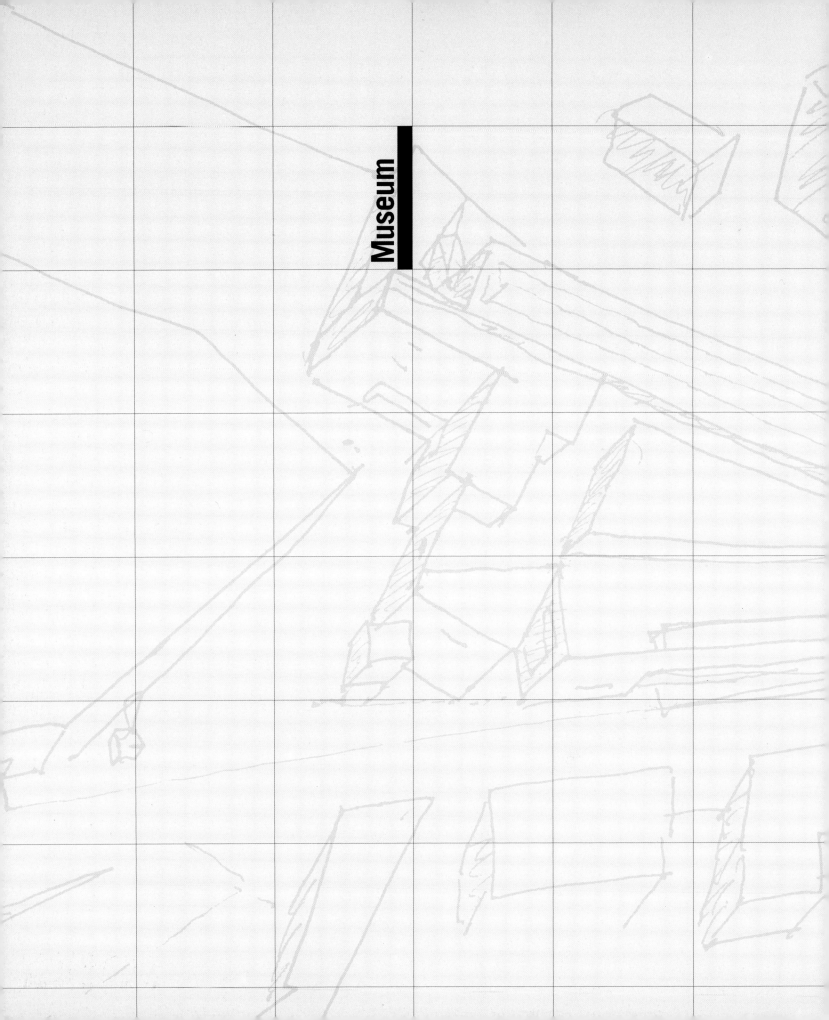

Museum

Santiago

Museum of Contemporary Art, Santiago de Compostela

The building of the Centro Gallego de Arte Contemporáneo (CGAC) in Santiago de Compostela, located within the ancient enclosure of the convent of Santo Domingo de Bonaval, contributes to the urban cohesion of a vast area that includes the convent of San Roque, the convent of Santo Domingo, the Porta do Caminho, the city quarter between As Rodas and Valle-Inclán streets, and the adjacent public spaces. It also serves as a unifying element for the various structures that came into being over time one after another in the absence of any overall plan dedicated to the whole. The CGAC was thus given the role of mediator in the complex existing relationships of scale and rank and the task of transforming a confused agglomerate of buildings and open spaces into a coherent urban construction.

The building complex is aligned along a north-south axis with a face on Valle-Inclán and a main entrance opposite the entrances to the convent and church of Santo Domingo. The compact form of the CGAC, which in one sense can be seen as a replacement for the enclosure wall that was demolished long ago, aligns in height with the eaves of the convent and church of Santo Domingo, thus emphasizing the church's importance within the context of the city while at the same time functioning as a sort of architectural hinge between the church buildings and adjacent structures. The guidelines of preservation and transformation adopted by the project involve in particular the choice of materials of facing. The external surfaces are faced in granite: this solution, dictated by climatic considerations and by the building tradition of Santiago, also makes it possible to enhance the constructive framework on which the

building is dependent, a structure in reinforced concrete with large openings. The building complex is composed of two bodies on three levels with a usable terrace; both bodies have an L-shaped ground plan (A to the west and B to the east); the two bodies converge and intersect at the southern end, forming a triangular interior space of the same height (C). The services called for in the project are distributed among all three bodies—A, B, and C, and the underground level extends beneath their combined area. Bodies A and C contain the services related to the exhibition halls (storerooms, laboratories, warehouses). Body B is comprised of the gallery that unites the complex's main vertical connections, as well as the rooms with the permanent displays. The public enters by way of a ramp parallel to Valle-Inclán Street that leads to the first level of the building: the entrance atrium, the reception area, and the foyer of the conference room are all located at this level in body A, and the rest area, the cafeteria, and the large hall for temporary exhibitions are in body B. The conference hall, in the short side of body B, can be reached both from the foyer and from the exhibition room. On the second level, the corresponding space in body B is given over to the exhibition halls of the center for documentation, which are illuminated by large shielded skylights, and by the reading room; body A's second level contains the administrative offices with their related service areas, which are connected to the lower floors by an internal stairway. The triangular space of body C is a transit area from which visitors can reach the exhibition rooms on all three levels. The roof terrace is open to the public and has an elevated belvedere offering panoramic views of the city and the garden below. It is set up for the presentation of sculpture exhibitions.

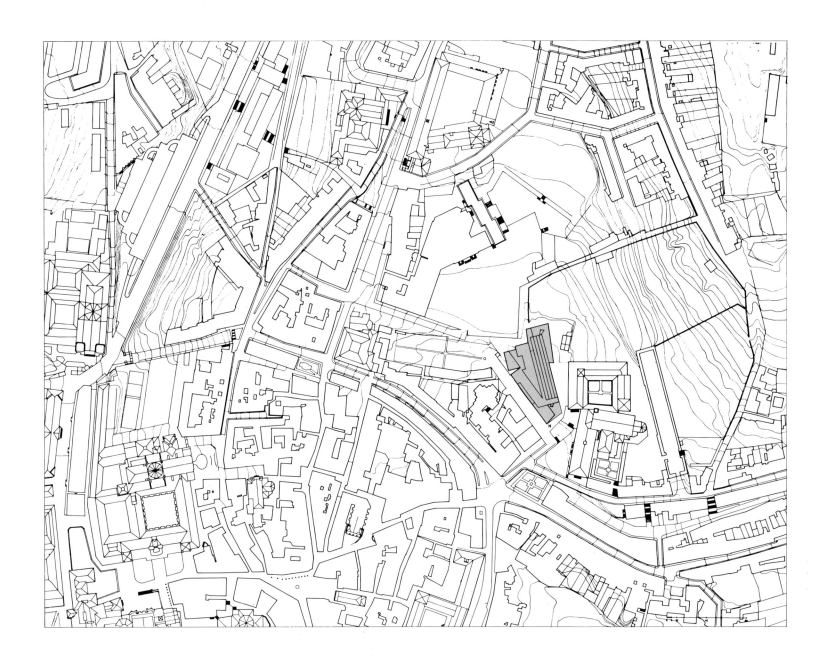

General plan of the city area (above).

The side facing Valle-Inclán Street with the
entrance ramp (opposite).

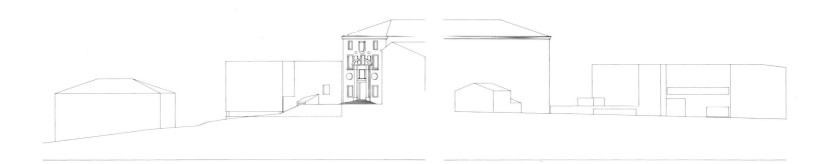

The side facing Valle-Inclán Street with the
entrance ramp (opposite).
Elevations of the south and east sides (top).
The south side facing the church (above).
Elevation of the face on Valle-Inclán Street with
the convent and church (opposite top).
The ramp and entrance (opposite center).
Scale drawing of the west side (opposite bottom).

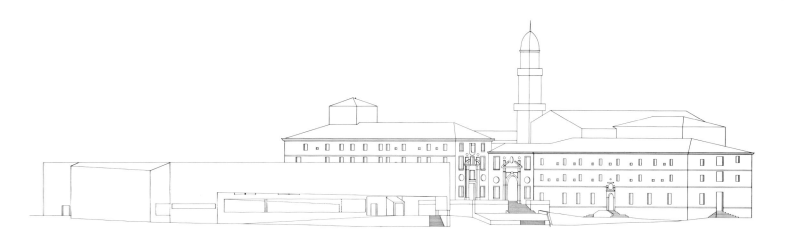

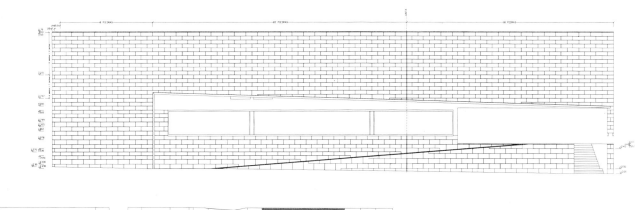

Views (above) of the entrance, a portion of
the west face, a hall, and an exhibition room.
Plan of the first floor (right).
Legend:
  1 entrance
  2 access ramp
  3 entrance portico
  4 atrium
  5 hall
  6 foyer
  7 conference room
  8 rooms for temporary exhibitions
  9 terrace of bar
10 bar
11 bookstore

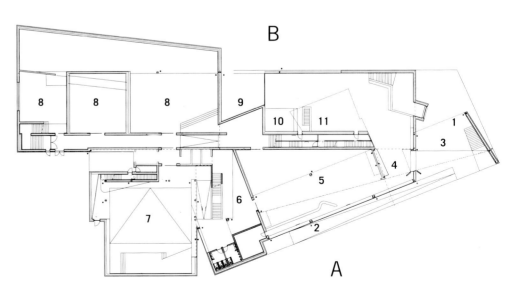

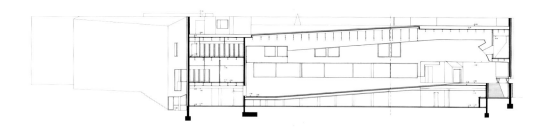

Cross section (top).
Views (above) of the atrium and the hall.
Plan of the second level (right).
Legend:
1 meeting room
2 offices
3 foyer
4 reading room
5 seminar room
6 exhibition room

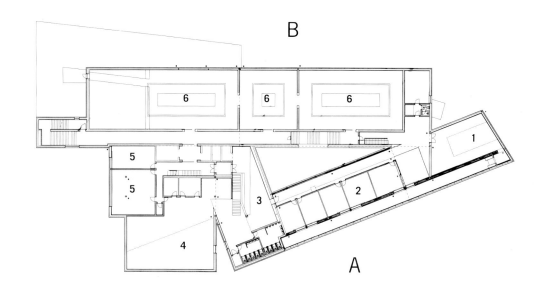

Santo Domingo de Bonaval Park, Santiago de Compostela

This project involved turning the ancient enclosure of the convent of Santo Domingo de Bonaval into a public garden, and it was accomplished with great respect for the original subdivision of the space. The main path through the park begins in the square formed by the church, the convent, and the entrance to the Centro Galleo de Arte Contemporáneo and runs alongside the eastern wall of the museum up to the area of the outdoor exhibitions. It then follows along the various levels across fields and orchards marked off by old walls before diverging into secondary paths that continue on to terraces with panoramic views, woods of oak trees, and bodies of water and irrigation canals, most of which had been completely forgotten before the project. The restoration of abandoned portals and the opening of new entrances have made it possible to enter the garden even from side streets and to reach the museum complex from the hill, where a restaurant and new parking facilities are planned in the future.

Entrance to the garden (above) and the terraces of the first and third levels (opposite).

Plan of the complex of Santo Domingo de Bonaval and the garden (left).
Legend:
1 museum of contemporary art
2 convent of Santo Domingo
3 former orchards of the convent
4 oak wood
5 former cemetery

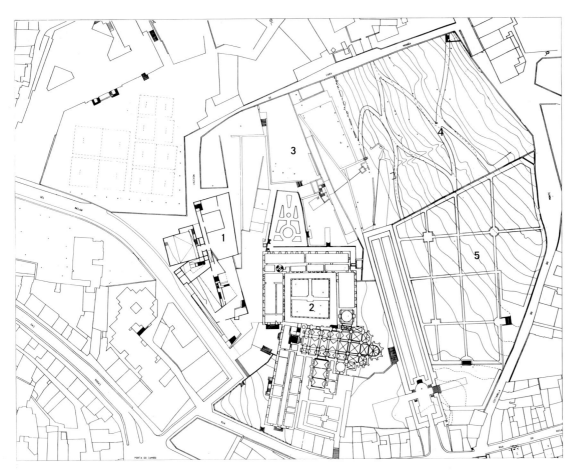

Two fountains (below and opposite).

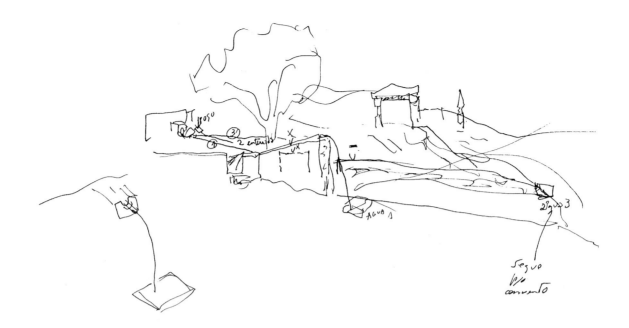

The area of the former orchard (above) and the
arcade on the terrace of the third level (opposite).

Ramps connecting the various levels of the
garden (below); views of the path alongside
the wall, and the entrance gate to the former
cemetery (opposite above).

Profile of the complex of Santo Domingo
de Bonaval (bottom).

PERFIL 1

RUA R DEL VALLE INCLAN

CENTRO GALEGO DE ARTE
CONTEMPORANEA

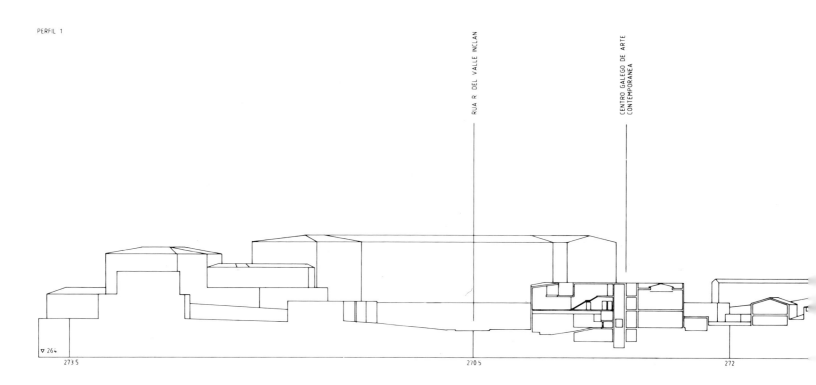

∇ 264

273 5

270 5

272

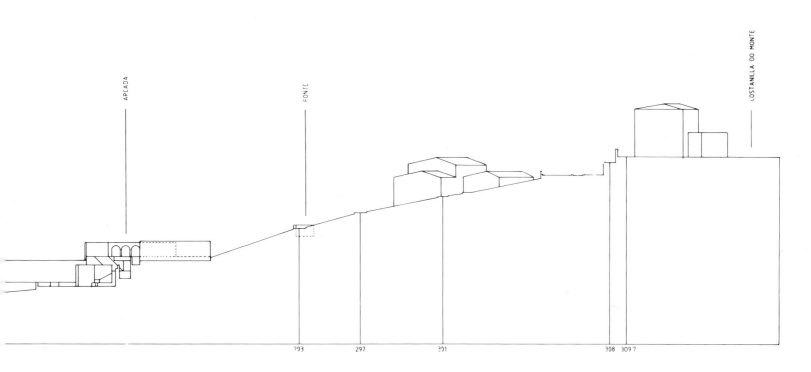

ARCADA

FONTE

COSTANILLA DO MONTE

293   297   301   308 309 7

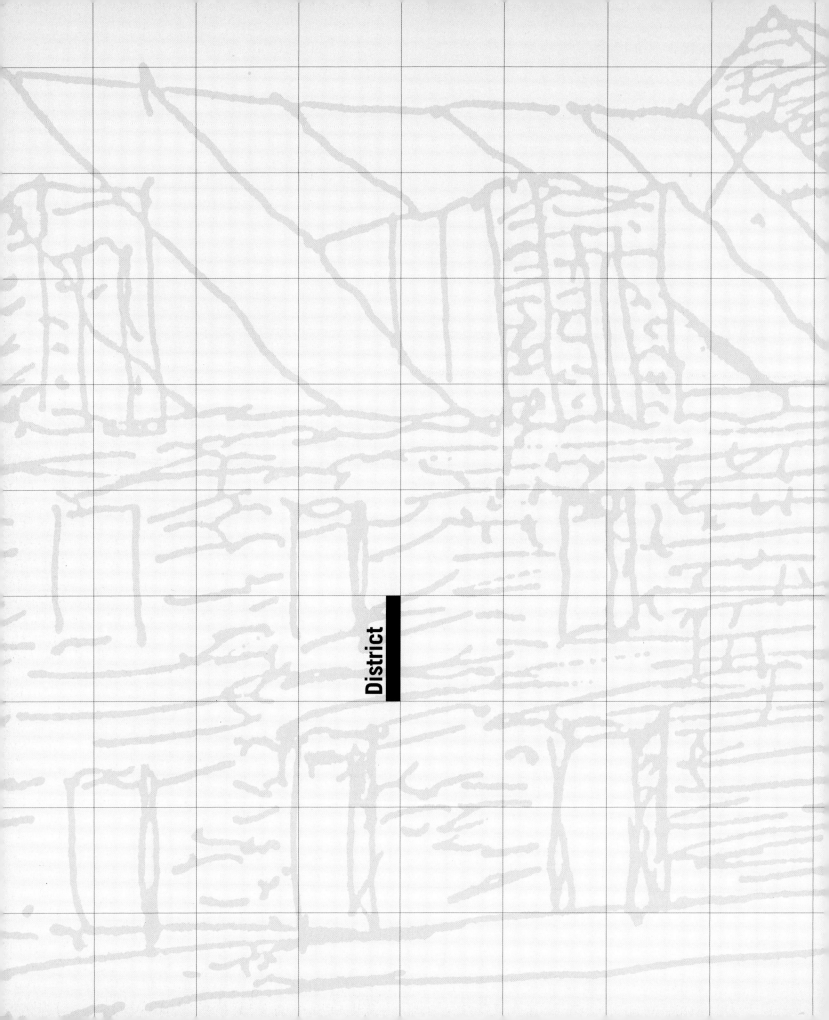

District

The Hague

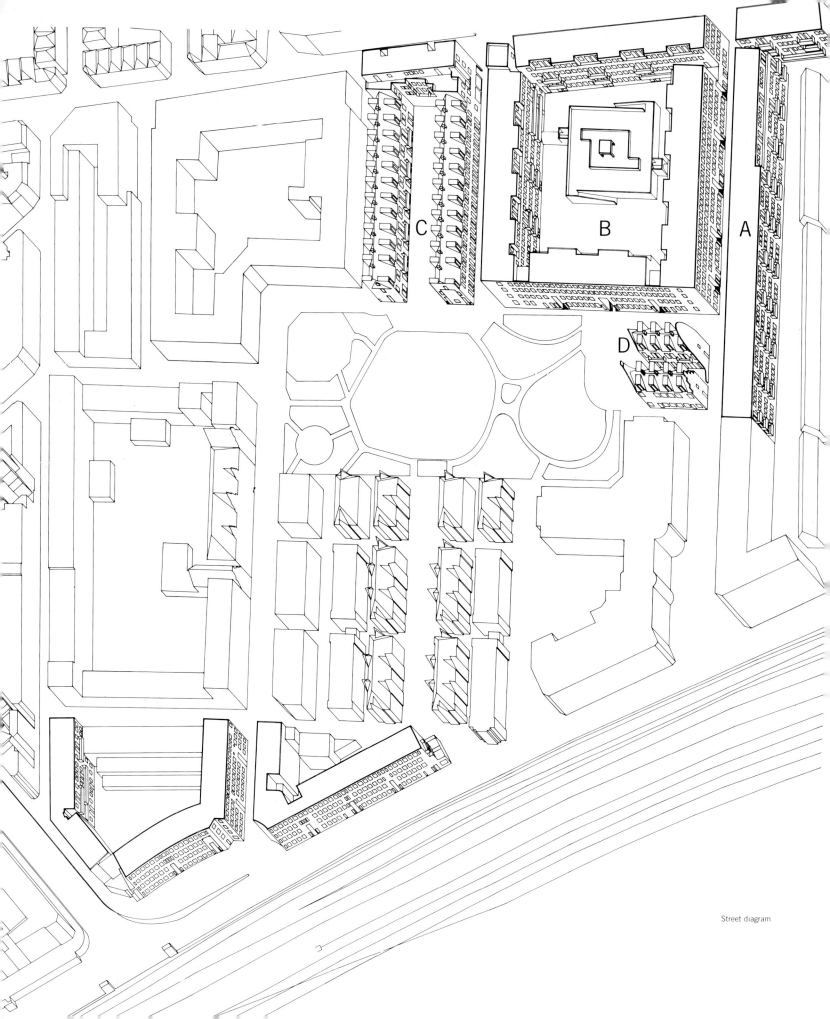

Street diagram

Housing Project, The Hague

Zone 5 of the Schilderswijk Centrum in The Hague—an area of popular housing built before the 1906 regulations and in large part demolished because of the poor state of the buildings—is the result of an urban renewal project worked out together with the city administration and the tenants' association (50 percent of the tenants are immigrants). It is thus an outstanding example of decision making by "committee" and is also proof that urban renovation can be accomplished while at the same time maintaining respect for tradition. The concept involves reorganizing the layout of the area and altering the sizes of the buildings and the common spaces. It also establishes the criteria to follow in order to preserve the district's specific character: streets lined by an unbroken row of building façades without projections but with regularly spaced openings; compact blocks of four-story residences with internal courtyards; when possible, direct, independent access to every apartment through a traditional "portico"; brick facings; signs painted in traditional colors; and a uniform roofing style.

Blocks A, B, C, and D are located on the northeast corner of the zone between Hoefkade Street, a major commercial artery, to the north, and Jacob van Campen Square to the south. As in the blocks already constructed on the opposite end of the district, between Maristraat and Paralleleweg, the apartments are entered in the way typical of houses in The Hague, with separate entries on the street level for the ground-floor homes and access stairs to the upper floors, with separate stairways from the second to the third floors and from the second to the fourth floors. The façades giving on to the courtyard are marked off by balconies resting on corbels of reinforced concrete.

The interior arrangement of the apartments is marked by the utmost flexibility so as to make the apartments adaptable to the needs of the different cultures of the inhabitants; large sliding doors are used to create greater flexibility within the inhabited space, such that kitchens that communicate with living rooms can be completely isolated, for example, using a sliding door. The kitchen and living room face on to the street; the bedrooms face the inner courtyard.

In addition to the gardens for the use of the inhabitants on the ground floor and the common garden, the courtyard in Block B has a parking garage that can be reached by way of separate passages opening to the east and west of the block itself, thus connecting with the interior streets of the district.

Photos by Lorenzo Mussi

The southern end of the buildings in Block C as
seen from the far side of Jacob van Campen Square.

Block A

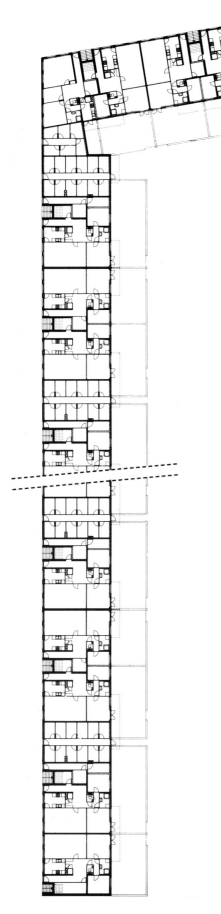

Plan of the ground floor of Block A (left) and diagrams of the apartments on the ground, second, third, and fourth floors (below).
Legend:
1 living room
2 kitchen
3 bedroom
4 bathroom
5 entrance

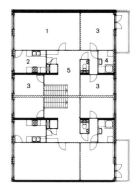

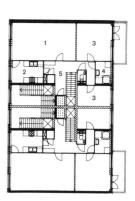

Block A between Hoefkade Street, to the
north, and Jacob Catsstraat, to the west.

The north end of Block A on Jacob Catsstraat (above), and
the north end of Block B on Hoefkade Street (opposite).

Block B

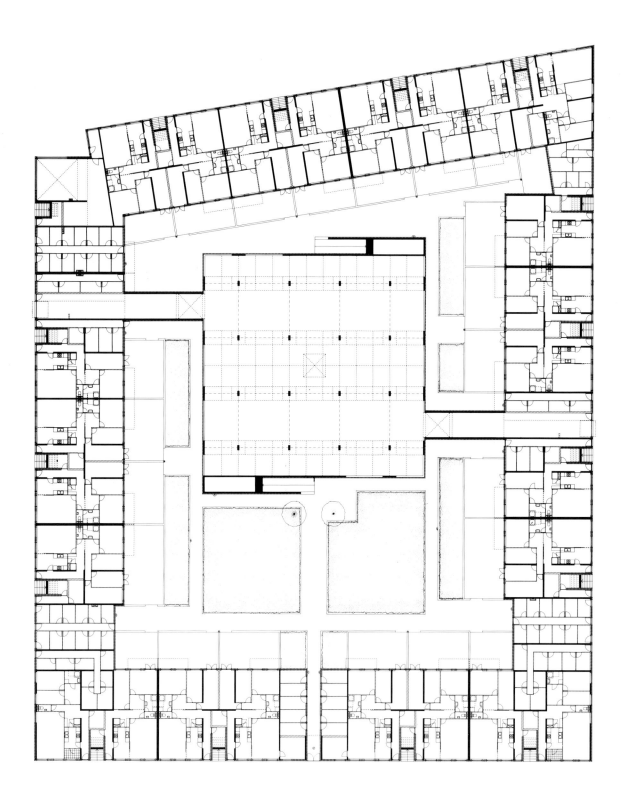

Plan of the ground floor of Block B.

Corner view of Block B showing the northern and eastern façades (above).
Diagrams showing Block B's inner façade on the courtyard (below) and its outer façade on the street (bottom).

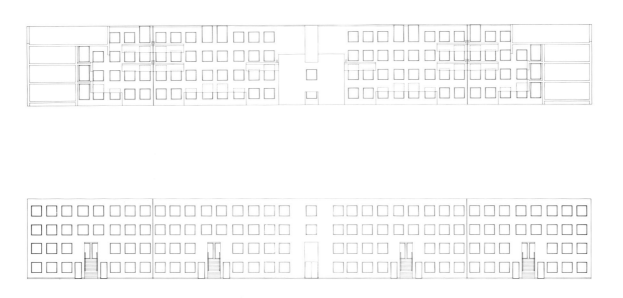

Corner view of Block B showing its northern and western façades (top).
Blocks B, A, and D as seen from Jacob van Campen Square (above).

The courtyard of Block B (top and above).

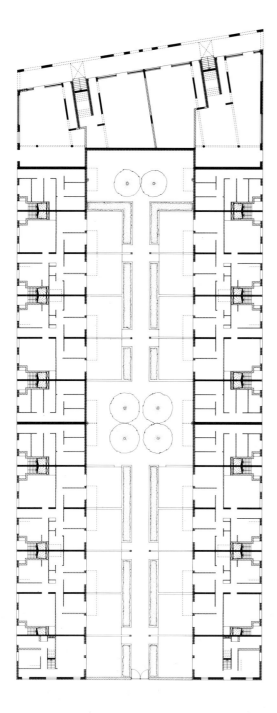
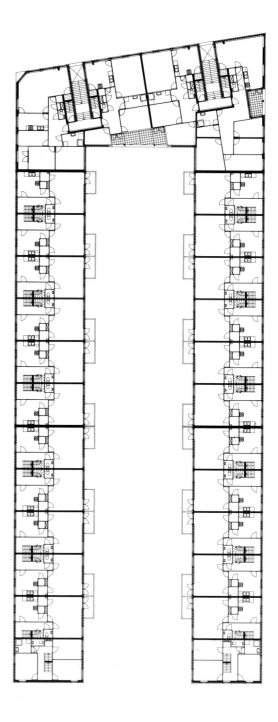

Plans of the ground floor (left)
and second floor (right) of Block C.

Views of Block C (opposite): the corner of
Hoefkade and Jan Steen streets (opposite top)
and the façade on Jacob van Campen Square
(opposite bottom).

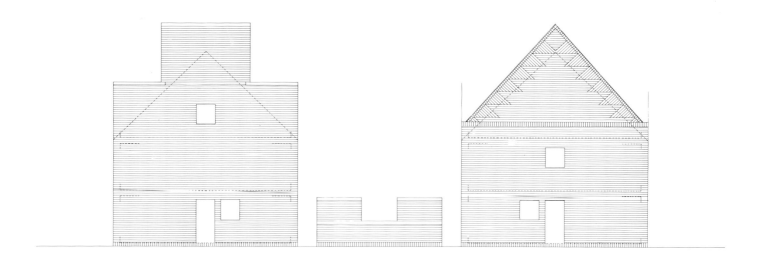

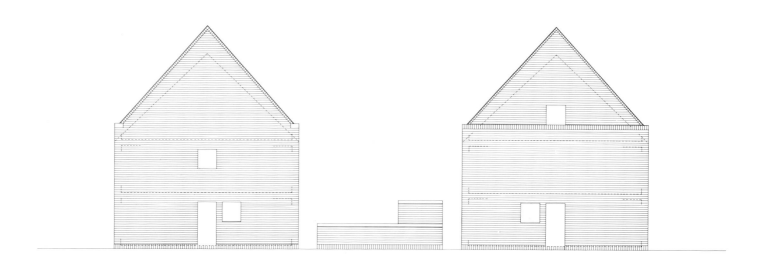

Drawings of the block from the side (above).
The façade on Jacob Catsstraat (opposite top).
Plans and cross sections of Block D (opposite bottom).

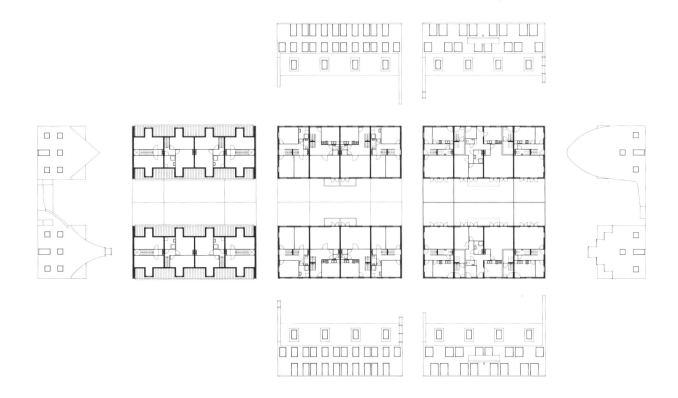

Blocks C, B, and D from
Jacob van Campen Square.

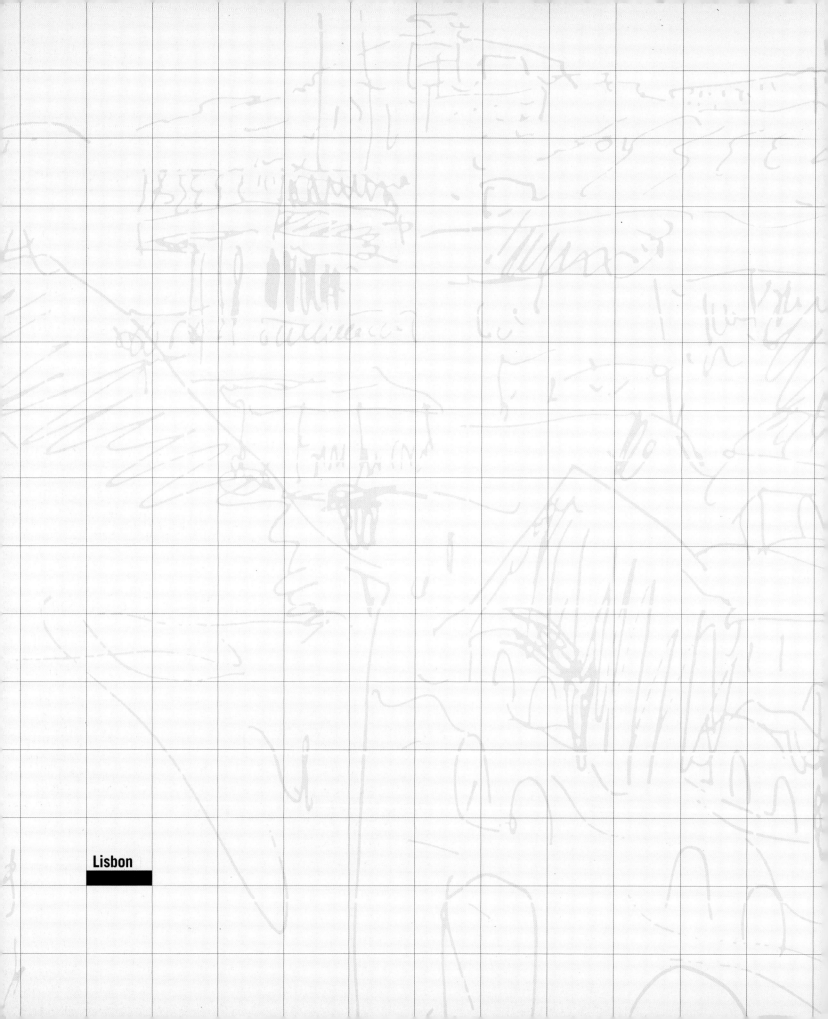

Lisbon

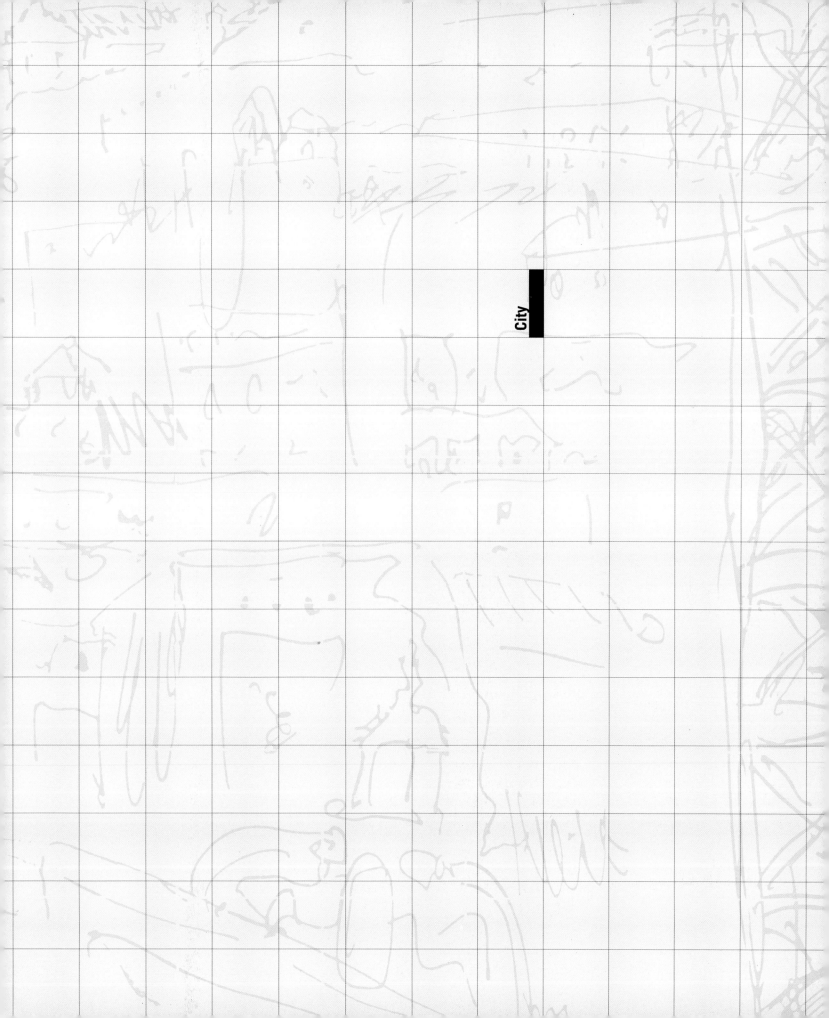

City

Reconstruction of the Chiado District, Lisbon

The Chiado district of Lisbon, located between the flat area of the Baixa Pombalina and the hill of the Bairro Alto, is a historic zone of great civic and commercial importance to the city. In August of 1988 seventeen buildings near the intersection of Nova Do Almado, Garrett, and Do Carmo streets were destroyed totally or partially by fire. Except for the large Chiado and Grandella department stores, the buildings in the district are of the Pombal type: austere architecture characterized by the regular spacing of windows and doors and extreme simplicity of ornamentation. The new plan for the rebuilding the district was designed to maintain as far as possible the original alignment of the buildings and the architectural characteristics of their façades, while making changes to the city blocks themselves—the internal arrangement of which had not been regulated by Pombal's plan—in order to create new public spaces and to open new streets and passageways ascending the hill and connecting with the subway station, thus establishing the necessary context for the planned revitalization of the district.

The plan for block A, a squarish area on several levels marked off by Garrett, Nova Do Almada, and Ivens streets and by a stairway on the fourth side, involved dividing the block into three parts organized according to residential and commercial functions, all giving on to a public patio created by expanding the old interior courtyard. Three pedestrian passageways were opened in the block to give access to this interior space. The buildings in block B face on to Garrett, Do Carmo, and Calcado Do Sacramento streets; here a pedestrian passageway with landings and steps was created along the route of an important medieval street, long abandoned, leading all the way to a small square opened opposite the portico of the Church of the Carmo,

located on the highest point of the Chiado district and still in ruins after the disastrous earthquake of 1755. Here as elsewhere reducing the depth of surroundings buildings permitted creation of public zones, where pedestrians can stop and meet. The Chiado Building, also known as the Barcelinhos Palace, was originally the Convento Do Espirito Santo da Pedreira; it was then an aristocratic residence before becoming the headquarters of the Chiado department store. Its original structure has remained substantially intact despite the alterations made following the changes in use and the damage from natural disasters. The rebuilding and consolidations of the new plan are designed to respect the late-baroque design of the building—it was never completed—created by José Joachim Ludovic, after which it will be turned into a hotel with an internal entrance to the subway station.

The Grandella Building—designed in 1900 by Georges Demay, the architect responsible for the Au Printemps department store in Paris—is located between Do Carmo and Aurea streets and Assunção Street to the south. It thus acts as a sort of hinge between the Baixa and the Bairro Alto. The new plan will do nothing to change this building's architectural style, which makes it stand out from the severe structures around it. In fact, its decorative elements, as intended by the marqués de Pompal, break the uniformity of the urban fabric; these include Art Nouveau-style door and window frames in hammered iron, stone façades with figurative decoration, elaborate stucco cornices, and large windows. Furthermore, its supporting structure is made of reinforced concrete, permitting great flexibility in the design of its internal spaces, which will be used for commercial and cultural activities, offices, and parking.

Nova Do Almada and Do Carmo streets as seen from a balcony on the Castro and Melo building (opposite). To the right is the Chiado Building of department stores.

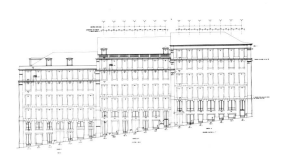
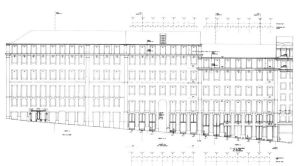

Sectional views of Nova Do Almada and Do Carmo streets before the fire and after the reconstruction (above).

Via Nova Do Almada (opposite). To the left are the Chaves and Casto and Melo buildings.

Map of the new plan
Legend:

Bldg. 1	arch. J. Branco
2	arch. José Esteves
3	arch. J. Busquets and A. Siza
4	arch. Álvaro Siza
5	-
6	arch. Álvaro Siza
7	arch. Álvaro Siza
8	arch. Álvaro Siza
9	arch. Simoes Tiago
10	arch. Teotónio Pereira
11	arch. Ana Salta
12	arch. Ana Salta
13-15	arch. José Esteves
16	arch. José Esteves
17	*
18	*
19	*
20	arch. Teotónio Pereira
21	*
22	*
23	*
24	*
25	*

* buildings not damaged by the fire

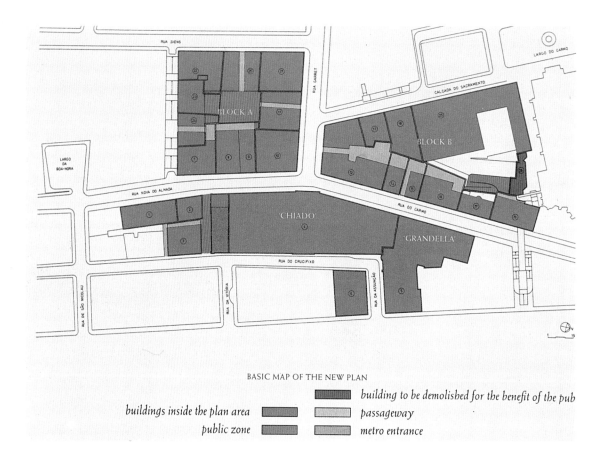

BASIC MAP OF THE NEW PLAN

buildings inside the plan area

public zone

building to be demolished for the benefit of the pub

passageway

metro entrance

Views (right and opposite top) of interiors in the Camara Chaves Building.

Plans of the duplexes on the sixth and seventh floors of the Camara Chaves Building (opposite bottom).

The public patio inside Block A (below).

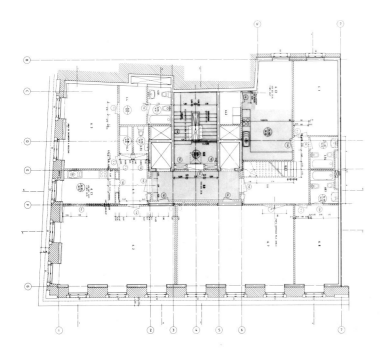
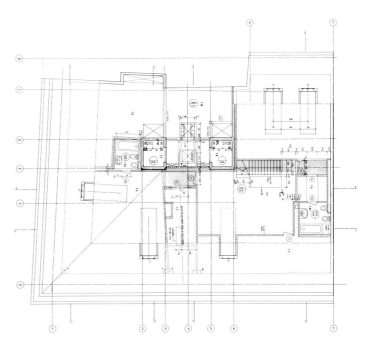

Views (above) of interiors in the Casto and Melo Building.

Plan of the sixth floor of the Casto and Melo Building and cross section of that Building.

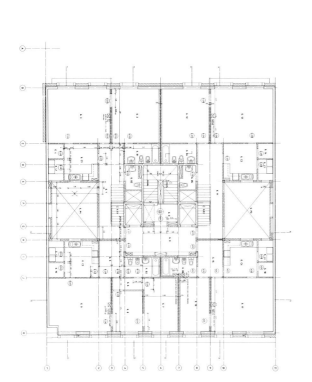
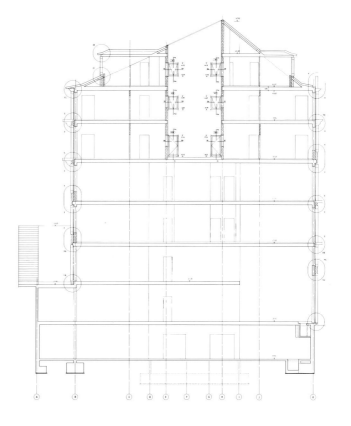

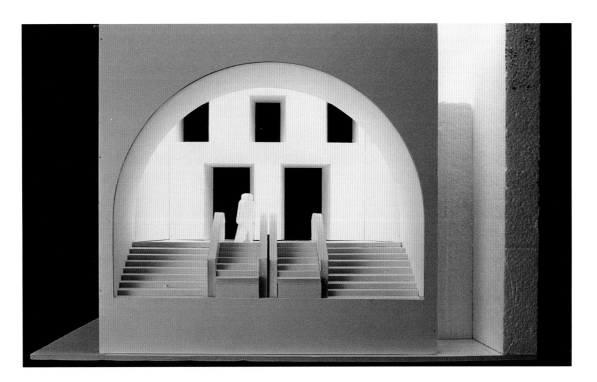

Models of the subway station.

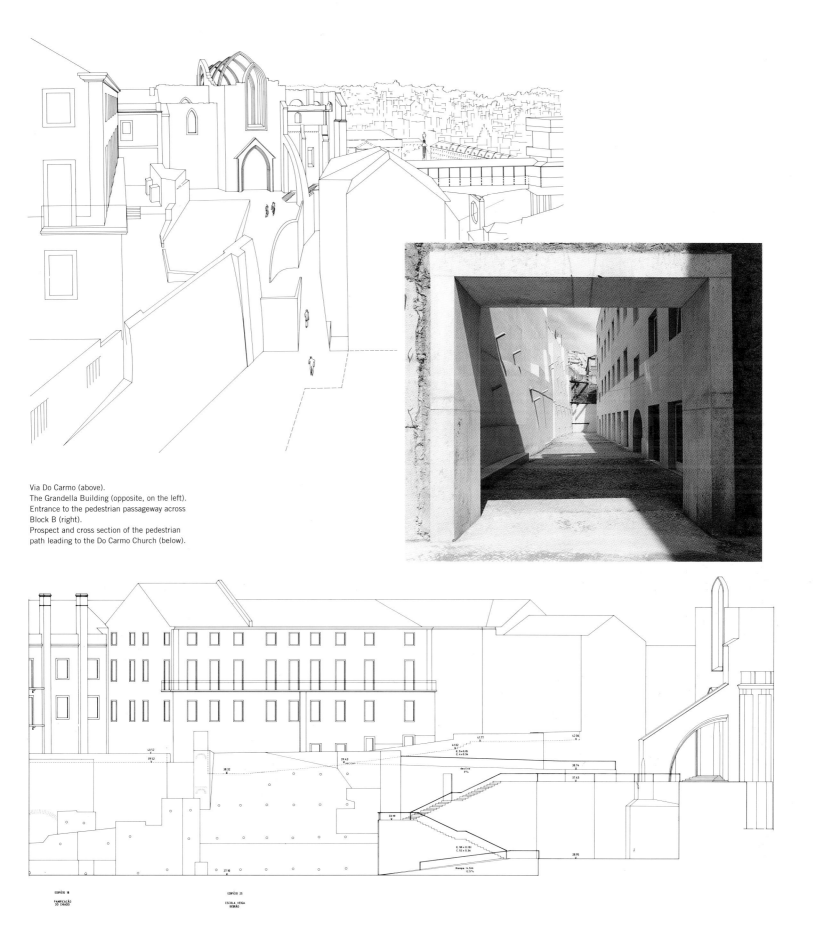

Via Do Carmo (above).
The Grandella Building (opposite, on the left).
Entrance to the pedestrian passageway across
Block B (right).
Prospect and cross section of the pedestrian
path leading to the Do Carmo Church (below).

Views of the Grandella Building: the roofline (above)
and interiors (opposite).

Álvaro (Joachim Melo) Siza Vieira was born in Matozinhos (near Oporto), Portugal, in 1933. He studied at the architecture school of the University of Oporto from 1949 to 1955 and completed his first building project in 1954. From 1955 to 1958 he worked as a staff member in the architectural studio of Fernando Távora. He taught in the architecture school of the University of Oporto (ESBAP) from 1966 to 1969, and in 1976 he was named professor of construction, which he still teaches today. He has taught as a visiting professor at the École Polytechnique of Lausanne, Pennsylvania University, the Los Andes University of Bogotá, and the Graduate School of Design of Harvard University. His many projects include 1,220 residences at the Quinta de Malagueria in Évora, the faculty of architecture of Oporto, the library of the University of Aveiro, and the meteorological center of the Olympic Village of Barcelona. Since 1985 he has been in charge of coordinating the urban renewal plan for the Schilder quarter of The Hague, and he has been directing the plan for the reconstruction of Lisbon's Chiado district since 1988. He is also in charge of the Praça de Espanha/Avenida Malhoa city plan in Lisbon. His works have been exhibited in Copenhagen (1975); Barcelona (1976); Venice's Biennial (1978); Milan (1979); the Museum of Architecture, Helsinki; the Alvar Aalto Museum, Finland (1982); the Georges Pompidou Center, Paris (1982); the Institute of Contemporary Arts, London (1983); the Stichting Wonen, Amsterdam (1983); the Technhische Hogenschool, Delft (1984); the University of Oporto and the Almada Negreiros Gallery, Lisbon (1984); the Paris Biennial (1985); the Massachusetts Institute of Technology, Cambridge (1985); the 9H Gallery, London (1986); the IBA, Berlin (1987); Columbia University, New York (1987); the Graduate School of Design of Harvard (1987); the Georges Pompidou Center, Paris (1990); the Ministerio de Obras Públicas, Madrid (1990); the Riba, London (1991); the Colegio de Architectos, Seville (1991); the Singel Gallery, Antwerp (1992); the Galeria Rui Alberto, Oporto (1993); the Ministerio de Obras Públicas, Madrid (1993); the Colegio de Architectos, Granada (1994); the Sala do Risco, Lisbon (1994); the Centro Gallego de Arte Contemporáneo, Santiago de Compostela; the convent of Santa Clara, San Marino; the Ticinese Society of Fine Arts, Mendrisio, Switzerland (1995); Copenhagen; the Town Hall of Matozinhos, at the Belém Cultural Center, Lisbon; and the Colegio de Architectos, Tenerife (1996).

He has participated in many competitions, including the competition for the Schlesisches Tor Residences, Berlin, 1980 (first prize); the restoration of Campo di Marte, Venice, 1985 (first prize); the redesign of the casino and Winkler Café, Salzburg, 1986 (first prize); Expo '92, Seville, 1986; "A Project for Siena," 1988; the Centro Cultural de la Defensa, Madrid, 1989 (first prize); the Bibliothèque de France, Paris, 1990; the Helsinki Museum, 1993. The awards he has been granted include the prize from the Art Critics International Association, Portugal section, 1982; the architecture prize of the Architects Association of Portugal, 1987; the gold medal for architecture from the Upper Council of the Order of Architects of Spain, the gold medal from the Aalto Foundation, and the European prize in architecture from the European Economic Community/Mies Van der Rohe Foundation, Barcelona, 1988; the Pritzker Prize from the Hyatt Foundation, Chicago, 1992; the national prize from the Architects Association of Portugal, 1993; and the Secil prize, Lisbon, 1996. He has been awarded honorary degrees from the University of Valencia in 1992; the École Polytechnique Fédéral of Lausanne in 1993; the University of Palermo, University Henandez Pelayo of Santander, and the University of Engineering in Lima in 1995.

Aveiro (Portugal), Water Tower, University of Aveiro
design and creation 1988–89
with Jorge Nuno Monteiro
collaborator J.P. Xavier
construction GOP (Gabinete de Organização e Projecto), eng. J. A. Sobreira
photography G. Chiaramonte
Ovar (Portugal), Avelino de Oliveira Duarte House
design and creation 1981–85
with Miguel Guedes de Carvalho
collaborator R. Gonçalves
photography G. Chiaramonte
Alicante (Spain), Administration Building, University of Alicante
project 1995/work completed 1997
with Elisiário Miranda, Luiz Martinez-Planelles
collaborators L. Diaz-Mauriño, C. Ferreirinha, H. Kassam, A. Morata Ortiz,
C. Sepana, A. Silva
construction J. L. Perez Molina
installation J. Sorbes Llorca
photography of models T. Siza
Santiago de Composetla (Spain), Centro Gallego de Arte Contemporáneo
design and creation 1988–93
with Joao Sabugueiro, Yves Stump
collaborators L. Cardoso, J.L. Carvalho Gomes, J. Considine, T. Faria, A. Graf,
C. Lau, E. Miranda, M. Nery, J. Nuno Monteiro, M. Trautman, J. P. Xavier
associate office for the preliminary project Joan Falgueras, collaborators A. Fibla,
J. Fossas, J. Genis, J. Maristany, J. C. Minguel, R. Soto, A. Trilla
construction Euroconsult
installation A. Costa Pereira, P. Quirós Faria
photography G. Chiaramonte
photography of models T. Siza
Santiago de Compostela (Spain), Santo Domingo de Bonaval Park
design and creation 1993–94
collaborators C. Castanheira, A. D'amico, C. Muro, N. Nery, J. Sabugueiro
landscape architect Isabel Aguirre
photography G. Chiaramonte
The Hague (Netherlands), Public Housing, Schilderswijk Ward
design and creation 1983–93
with Carlos Castanheira
collaborators M. C. Bastai, J. Considine, T. Faria, C. Ferreirinha, J. van Groenewoud,
C. Guedes, P. Pacozzi, G. Páris Couto, A. Silva
associate offices Van der Broeck en Bakema; Geurst & Schulze Architekten
collaborators R. Bosch, T. Haydeen, R. van de Ven, H. de Clercq, E. de Jong,
R. van Loen
construction Ingeniersbureau Goudstikker, De Vries, Zoetermeer
photography L. Mussi
Lisbon (Portugal), Reconstruction of the Chiado District
design and creation 1988–96
with Carlos Castanheira, Jorge Carvalho, Luis Mendes, Avelino Silva
collaborators for the project and the building code A. Angelillo, M. C. Bastai,
A. Braga, C. Ferreirinha, A. Graf, J. van Groenewoud, C. Guedes, E. Miranda,
J. Nuno Monteiro, G. Páris Couto
collaborators for the architectural development and arrangement of external spaces
S. Almeida, M. Becker, M. C. Bastai, J. Carvalho, C. Castanheira, R. Castro, P. Cody,
S. Coelho, C. Gaenshirt, A. Graf, L. Mendes, C. Menéres Semida, C. Murray,
A. Noites, P. Pacozzi, C. Porcu, J. E. Rebelo, J. Sabugueiro
landscape architecture João Gomes da Silva
coordination and technical assistance on worksites Chiado Office, City of Lisbon
construction STA Segadães Tavares Associados Lda
installation Fernando Alvim; GFT, eng. Alfredo Costa Pereira
photography G. Chiaramonte

Printed and bound in Italy by Arti Grafiche Motta, Milano.